THE SPECTRUM OF
POLITICAL ENGAGEMENT

DAVID L. SCHALK

◊◊◊◊◊◊◊◊◊◊◊◊

The Spectrum of
Political Engagement

◊◊◊◊◊◊◊◊◊◊◊◊

MOUNIER, BENDA,
NIZAN,
BRASILLACH,
SARTRE

PRINCETON UNIVERSITY PRESS

Copyright © 1979 by Princeton University Press
Published by Princeton University Press, Princeton, New Jersey
In the United Kingdom:
Princeton University Press, Guildford, Surrey

All Rights Reserved
Library of Congress Cataloging in Publication Data will be
found on the last printed page of this book

Publication of this book has been aided by a grant from
The Andrew W. Mellon Foundation

This book has been composed in VIP Bembo

Clothbound editions of Princeton University Press books
are printed on acid-free paper, and binding materials are
chosen for strength and durability.

Printed in the United States of America by
Princeton University Press, Princeton, New Jersey

For Elisabeth, Laura, and Peter

Contents

◇◇◇◇◇◇◇◇◇

Preface

◊◊◊◊◊◊◊◊◊

"Engagement" is a French term which has been adopted into English because there is no precise equivalent in our language. Almost everything about engagement is controversial, including its proper definition.[1] Broadly we may define it as political involvement, usually by members of the intellectual class.

The problem of engagement first came to my attention when I was studying the particular case of the French novelist Roger Martin du Gard (1881-1958). Martin du Gard frequently dealt with historical and ideological questions in his novels. *Jean Barois* (1913) is focused on the Dreyfus Affair and *Summer 1914* (1936), the seventh part of Martin du Gard's massive *roman fleuve, Les Thibault*, concentrates exclusively on the coming of the First World War. Albert Camus believed that *Les Thibault* could legitimately be viewed as the first of the *romans engagés*.[2]

Martin du Gard was, however, firmly committed to the position that the artist should speak out only indirectly through his creative work, that political involvement, the signing of manifestoes, etc., usually leads to a lowering of literary quality and has no perceptible effect on the course of events. He expressed these views with such conviction that most critics and biographers believed he never descended into the political arena.

I began to suspect that Martin du Gard's relationship to engagement was more complex than it first appeared when I discovered that different writers cited different articles or public statements as being the sole exception to Martin du Gard's general rule of abstention. It eventually became clear that Martin du Gard had frequently been *engagé*, that since 1931, and perhaps even earlier, his passionate interest in contemporary affairs had led him into active commitment. A few months before his death in 1958, Martin du Gard joined

André Malraux, François Mauriac, and Jean-Paul Sartre in signing a petition protesting the seizure of Henri Alleg's book, *The Question*, and calling upon the government to renounce the use of torture in the Algerian War.[3] It is now accepted that Martin du Gard was not a totally withdrawn, "ivory-tower" artist.[4]

Martin du Gard's anguished fluctuations, his unwilling, sometimes hidden engagement, aroused my curiosity about other French intellectuals. Were any general patterns discernible? Who had formulated the concept of engagement, and when? I soon discovered that I had undertaken what a French colleague described as *un beau projet, mais si vaste et si délicat à traiter.* . . .[5]

Yet there was a special immediacy about my topic that made me press on. Just as I was beginning my research a new wave of engagement became visible. It seems to have originated in England in 1957, but unquestionably took on momentum in America with the Greensboro Sit-Ins of 1960.[6] It gained strength with the Port Huron Manifesto of 1962 which launched the Students for a Democratic Society as a national organization, and reached the universities with the Free Speech Movement at Berkeley in 1964. By the late 1960s the wave had spread to Europe and beyond, and in 1968, when the May Movement nearly brought France to a standstill, it returned to its linguistic homeland with a vengeance.

An earlier version of Chapter II was written when engagement was still a serious matter on university campuses and downtown streets,[7] and a book completed in those heady days would have been very different from the one I have written. But historical events do not often wait upon the whim of academics, and the wave of engagement crested in 1970 and declined precipitously after 1972. By 1978, the "American Intellectual Elite,"[8] has become almost totally quiescent, and passivity and a new professionalism dominate the university scene here. The picture in Europe is not that much different; troubles in the universities there appear to stem from uncertainty over career possibilities rather than political or ideological commitment.

Whether the current calm means the permanent end of engagement is a tantalizing though enormously difficult question, because it rests upon so many variables.[9] In any case I am writing about a phenomenon which has no immediate reality and thus theoretically can examine engagement with a dispassionate eye. The passage of time should provide the cushion of objectivity the historian needs. However, it is still difficult to be neutral about engagement. Personal bias, always a problem in intellectual history, is especially hard to eliminate when dealing with a concept that both powerfully attracts and repels intellectuals themselves. When we are *engagé*, we fear that we are debasing our highest values; when we are not, we worry that we have become, in Paul Nizan's trenchant phrase, mere *chiens de garde*.[10]

The word is French, and the concept of engagement as we have come to understand it was first articulated in France. Hence the emphasis in this book is on French intellectuals and their struggle to come to grips with the issues raised by engagement in the critical quarter-century which began in the aftermath of one costly and painful victory. The end of the period is marked by a second victory, which found France more intact physically but less spiritually.[11] Keeping broadly within these geographical and temporal limitations, I shall examine engagement—its origins, the arguments that have been used to denounce it and to defend it, its differing manifestations, and its effects, if any, on the "real" world of sociopolitical actuality. Many intellectuals who were politically active in the 1920–1945 period are discussed in this book, though four, who cover the full political spectrum and at first seem unlikely companions, are given the most attention. Moving from the left they are a communist (Paul Nizan), a left Catholic (Emmanuel Mounier), a democratic idealist (Julien Benda), and a fascist (Robert Brasillach). Jean-Paul Sartre, often erroneously viewed as the first to formulate the doctrine of engagement, is a special case and is discussed in the Epilogue. They all knew each other, and their attitudes toward each other ranged from violent hatred to grudging respect. Their very diversity makes their engagement fascinat-

ing; during the 1930s they all entered actively and energeti-
cally into the realm of politics.

I am indebted to the Old Dominion Foundation for a fellow-
ship which permitted me to undertake this project, and to the
National Endowment for the Humanities for a Summer
Stipend which enabled me to bring it to completion. Friends
and colleagues too numerous to mention have been generous
with help and advice, especially in bringing to my attention
source materials on the roots of engagement. I am grateful to
Angus Cameron for his encouragement and wise suggestions.
The staff of the Vassar College Library deserves special
thanks, as do Leili Parts and Norma Torney for helping with
the bibliography.

The late Edeltraut Proske Barrett, herself an *emigré* from
Europe in the 1930s, had an intuitive understanding of much
of what is discussed in this book. She was a constant inspiration, and I deeply regret that she did not live to read and
criticize the finished manuscript.

My wife Elisabeth has taken time from her own career to
argue countless points with me, and she has developed a
healthy scepticism about the pretensions of some *engagé* intellectuals, past and present. This book has benefited from her
critical eye, though she is in no way responsible for any of its
contents.

Finally, I should like to thank R. Miriam Brokaw and Mar-
got Cutter of Princeton University Press. Their efficiency,
keen judgment, and prompt cooperation have eased every
step in preparing this work for publication. An author could
not ask for more.

All translations, unless otherwise indicated, are my own. In
certain key passages, where it is important that the translation
be as precise as possible, I have also included the original
French.

D. L. S.

Poughkeepsie, New York
May 1978

THE SPECTRUM OF
POLITICAL ENGAGEMENT

I

◊◊◊◊◊◊◊◊

What Was Engagement?

◊◊◊◊◊◊◊◊

INTRODUCTION

> We are not the bearers of consciousness. We are the
> whores of reason.
>
> Jan Myrdal[1]

The perennial modern controversy over intellectuals in politics has perhaps never been more succinctly articulated than in
this passage from the autobiography of Gunnar Myrdal's brilliant and disaffected son. Are those who remain uninvolved in
truth the "whores of reason," or are they the "bearers of consciousness"? Probably this controversy will continue as long
as there is a social group which can, with some degree of
legitimacy, be termed the intellectual class. The issue is
fraught with potential for ideological conflict. By considering
the word "engagement" we should be able to circumvent, or
at least suspend, this conflict. "Engagement" was first used in
scholarly studies after its importation from France, but has
now gained wide enough acceptance to find its way into the
New York Times, *Time Magazine*, and *Newsweek*.[2] The vaguer
term "commitment" is sometimes used, but "engagement"
most closely describes the political involvement that elicits so
much debate in intellectual circles.

The primary aims of this chapter will be to examine both
the origins and the definition of "engagement." By pursuing
these goals rather single-mindedly we can minimize polemics
while clarifying our understanding of some of the difficult
questions relating to intellectuals in politics. If we can satisfac-

torily answer the question "What was Engagement?" we should be able to appreciate better the arguments for and against it.

Turning first to official definitions, a review of French dictionaries and encyclopedias dating from the nineteenth century to the 1920s shows that as many as thirteen different definitions of engagement were delineated, but that none had any political bearing. With the 1961 edition of the *Grand Larousse encyclopédique*, however, two of the fourteen definitions given are political. The first is a simple statement: "Action of taking sides in political or social matters: The engagement of a writer." (It is interesting that the Larousse editor chose as a specific example a member of an intellectual profession.) A sentence from Cocteau is selected to illustrate the proper use of the word. "I am a neutralist. I hesitate when confronted with engagement."

In a second paragraph, the Larousse encyclopedia expands its definition by asserting that engagement is both contemporary and universal. One could argue, the editor adds, that there has always been a conflict of duties provoked by political, social, and ideological struggles, and that in this sense one could speak of the engagement of Antigone. (Another example would be Socrates, and a case could be made that he was the first *engagé* intellectual about whom much is known.) The word engagement, the Larousse editor continues, has been given a certain metaphysical content because of its adoption by existentialism. Jean-Paul Sartre's contribution is mentioned, but no reference is made to Paul Nizan or Emmanuel Mounier, the other two writers most responsible for defining and popularizing the concept.[3] The article on engagement concludes by noting that the word is "usually applied to intellectuals (thinkers, writers, artists), because it seems that their taking a position is more willed [*voulue*] than that of other social categories." The second reason the editor gives for applying engagement preferably to intellectuals is that they are always free to move off onto a track of "art for art, gratuitous literature, disinterested thought," and that if they do not, it is because they have chosen engagement.

It would seem that following Larousse we can accept the basic definition of engagement as the action of intellectuals, primarily in the political sphere. Other social groups, such as the workers (in Europe at least) would be automatically engaged, and applying the term to workers would be pleonastic. The word seems to suit best groups which do not normally feel obliged to speak out on public issues, to take action in one form or another. An ingredient of will and of thought and thus freedom is involved in the response to events, rather than a visceral reaction of immediate self-defense. In other words, engagement cannot occur when one is literally, physically, forced to be involved.

THE ROOTS OF ENGAGEMENT

The definition we have derived is still only operational and descriptive, and to expand it further we shall first have to turn to a closely related question, "When and how did the term engagement come to be used?" Of course the phenomenon we now describe as engagement occurred long before the twentieth century. As far as individuals are concerned, Antigone and Socrates have already been mentioned, and one could add Dante, Machiavelli, St. Thomas More, and many others. Groups of intellectuals such as the *philosophes* and the romantics have been shown to have been *engagé*.[4] For our purposes, however, the best place to begin is with the Dreyfus Affair, where the roots of so many crucial twentieth-century developments have been located.[5] The significance of the Dreyfus Affair specifically for intellectual history has been widely recognized, and Michel Winock's claim that "the Dreyfus Affair was the epic genesis of the French intellectuals" is not exaggerated.[6]

Julien Benda once wrote, "For the *clerc*, the Dreyfus Affair is the palladium of history."[7] It is but one of the paradoxes surrounding engagement that Benda, whose most famous

work, *La Trahison des clercs* (1927), is usually interpreted as a
polemic against engagement, began his long public career by
plunging ardently into the Affair on the side of the Drey-
fusards. Benda was by no means an isolated case, for the
Dreyfus Affair marks the first systematic and organized political involvement on the part of a group of individuals posses-
sing a self-conscious identity as intellectuals. In fact it was not
until the Dreyfus crisis reached a sort of climax with the publication of Emile Zola's *J'Accuse*, in January 1898, that the
noun *intellectuel* became a part of everyday French vocabulary.[8] As David L. Lewis has written, "After *J'Accuse* the role
of the man of letters in France and eventually in Western society was irrevocably altered."[9] The collective action on the
part of the intellectual supporters and opponents of Dreyfus
may have been "Engagement Willy-Nilly," or "Engagement
in Spite of Oneself," as the Dutch scholar H. L. Wesseling has
argued in a provocative essay.[10] But it was engagement
nonetheless, as Wesseling amply documents through a careful
statistical evaluation of three thousand individuals who signed
the "Manifeste des Intellectuels" in Clemenceau's Dreyfusard
newspaper *L'Aurore*.

In his excellent introductory study of the Dreyfus Affair,
Pierre Miquel takes a slightly different approach to the roots
of engagement. Miquel credits the intellectuals with trans-
forming the "Case" into the "Affair" and then into a
"Myth." Great journalists like Clemenceau and Rochefort
could utilize the press to serve their own ends, but they were
unable, Miquel claims, to raise the level of the debate.

> Only the entry into the lists of men like Péguy, Jaurès
> (*sic*), Lucien Herr, Barrès, Brunetière, could transform a
> quarrel into an extraordinary confrontation of ideas. . . .
> Those who were called, with a new name, the "Intellec-
> tuals," knew how to confer to the debate a formal moral
> dignity which it had lacked.[11]

An important positive result of the Dreyfus Affair was,
Miquel believes, to establish the role of intellectuals in public

life, to drive them from their libraries. "The massive and spontaneous engagement of professors, of writers, of artists, made it brilliantly clear that it had become impossible to govern men while betraying the laws of the spirit. Thought itself took on the awareness of having real power in a democracy."[12]

Both Wesseling and Miquel have broadened the encyclopedia definition of engagement by adding the element of group involvement. They have also, from a strict etymological point of view, made a technical error, in that they have linked the very notion of "intellectual," just as it was coming into existence during the Dreyfus Affair, with the concept of "engagement." As will be shown in the third part of this chapter, "engagement" began to be used in its modern sense of political involvement only in the 1930s. Worrying about this anachronism could be dismissed as pedantic quibbling, and indeed *engagé* intellectuals would be especially prone to do so. They would find it more tempting to examine Miquel's intriguing assertion that the Dreyfus Affair proved that the engagement of intellectuals can have an actual influence on events. However, such an inquiry, fascinating as it might become, would quickly bog down in polemic,[13] if we do not attempt to set engagement in its proper historical context and search for a more precise definition. Should we include all political involvement of intellectuals, acting both as individuals and in groups, in all historical periods under the rubric of engagement, or should we look for more specific kinds of behavior?

A way to approach engagement historically is suggested by Louis Bodin, who has written a valuable survey of the intellectual class. Bodin observes, quite correctly, that during the 1930s and especially in 1944-1945, many authors insisted on "the necessity of the engagement of the intellectual." More recently, opposition has developed, and some writers have advocated *dégagement*. Bodin, writing in 1964, viewed the quarrel over engagement as no longer fruitful, since it is now widely recognized that "there exists no intellectual who does not hold explicit or implicit positions toward the society in which he lives, and that it does not suffice for a person to adopt political positions to be qualified as an intellectual." In any case, Bodin believes, the debate over engagement marks an "important episode in French cultural history."[14]

It would be easy to enlarge upon Bodin's conclusion since the debate over engagement has clearly not been limited to the boundaries of France. One could even argue that because of its growing sophistication the debate over engagement was one of the most important new developments in European, perhaps also American, cultural and intellectual history of the period 1920-1945. The intensity and duration of engagement, and the number of intellectuals involved, increase dramatically in these years. This was the generation of "Writers on the Left," "The God that Failed," and "The Appeal of Fascism," not to mention "The Intellectual Migration," and many facets of this unusually high level of intellectual political involvement have already been studied.[15] This involvement was in large measure a response to the rise of totalitarianism, with its concomitant violence, persecutions, and heightened ideological conflict. In the context of intellectuals in politics, the Spanish Civil War emerges as probably the single most crucial event, what Stuart Samuels has called a "central force and a cohesive symbol," a "rallying point for all on the left. . . . Spain lifted the intellectual anti-fascist cause into a cause for justice."[16] Intellectuals on the right, though far fewer in number, were also drawn into the conflict in Spain.[17] It would be appropriate to turn from Spain to the period of the German Occupation and the Resistance, 1940-1944, which could be seen as the peak of engagement, at least in France and the rest of Occupied Europe. "We were never freer than under the German Occupation," wrote Jean-Paul Sartre. This was the moment when "each of our gestures carried the weight of an engagement."[18] François Mauriac, for once rather close to Sartre, spoke of the Resistance as a time "of true communion, I would also say a time of great hope. Never have I hoped so much as at that moment."[19]

In examining engagement from this more limited perspective, one might note the irony that by the time Sartre theorized about it in 1948 in his famous *Qu'est-ce que la littérature?* (*Situations*, II), its reality if not its necessity had faded. Emmanuel Mounier (1905-1950), the founder of the periodical *Esprit* and an early proponent of engagement, remarked after the Second World War that it is "because people do not engage themselves enough that there is today so much discussion of engagement. . . ."[20]

Following the more narrowly historical approach suggested by Pierre Miquel leads to the conclusion that since 1945 the phenomenon of engagement has been on the decline, save for occasional spurts of activity, for example in France during the Algerian War (1954-1962), or in America in the late 1960s.

How then did "engagement" come to be used in its modern sense? Can we trace the concept itself back to its roots? In examining these questions one soon discovers that there is substantial disagreement over priorities, a kind of *quérelle de précédence*. Academics love such disputes, and have thrived on them at least since the Renaissance. There is an added complication here because *engagé* intellectuals often dismiss these kinds of arguments as sterile, myopic, and irrelevant. They might, however, feel obliged to make an exception for this particular case, since it touches them so directly.

Two points can be resolved fairly quickly, after which complications develop. First, engagement as a term describing certain kinds of behavior was delineated by left-leaning intellectuals, and has more frequently, though by no means uniquely, been used to designate political involvement on the left. Secondly, the rather widely held opinion that Jean-Paul Sartre in *What is Literature?* and other writings of the immediate postwar period initiated the discussion of engagement cannot be sustained. The British author Maxwell Adereth represents this common view clearly when he states that *What is Literature?*, the "Bible of French commitment," is the "first serious attempt to define 'engagement.' "[21] In fact, Sartre drew heavily in *What is Literature?* from a work by his close friend and former roommate at the *Ecole Normale Supérieure*, Paul Nizan. The work in question is *Les Chiens de garde* (*The Watchdogs*), published in 1932. The complex and fascinating relationship between these two intellectuals, who were frequently mistaken for each other by third parties, and were sometimes called "Nitre et Sarzan," has been astutely analyzed by W. D. Redfern.[22] The degree of influence Nizan has had on Sartre is very striking and is not yet widely recognized, though Sartre performed a sort of *mea culpa* in his long introduction to the new edition of Nizan's *Aden Arabie* (1960). Jean-Albert Bédé, a classmate of the two men at the *Ecole Normale* and later a professor at Columbia University, wrote in 1967, almost thirty years after Nizan's death, that Nizan's career "precedes and, in an important measure, governs that of Sartre—through the effect of an emulation which still continues and of which there are few examples in the history of ideas."[23]

One example of the lack of general awareness of the degree of Nizan's influence on Sartre comes from Adereth's book, *Commitment in Modern French Literature*. Adereth writes that "Sartre even says that abstention is a form of commitment because it implies acceptance of the status quo."[24] This argument, often used to defend engagement, is stated at least three times in *Les Chiens de garde*, perhaps most succinctly as "Abstention is a choice."[25] And further, to show how difficult it is to trace an idea to its origins, Romain Rolland, in an open letter to Gerhart Hauptmann, dated August 29, 1914, writes urging his German colleague to join him in a public protest against the German invasion of Belgium, ". . . in such a moment, silence itself is an act" (*en un pareil moment, le silence même est un acte*).[26]

Sartre is also predated by the Catholic personalists, who had been using the term engagement, again since 1932, when *Esprit* was founded under the editorship of Emmanuel Mounier. Mounier and the other contributors to *Esprit* de-

serve credit for persistent reference to engagement, and for a
number of efforts to delineate its significance. By 1943-1947,
it had become one of the favorite terms in the writings of the
worker-priests.[27] However, we must be careful not to assign
all the honor (or blame, and there are to be sure many academics, not to mention clerics and politicians, who oppose
engagement) to Mounier and the personalists.

Candide Moix, who has written the first major study of
Mounier's life and work, believes that Mounier *was* the first
to use the term in France, and that it had originally come from
Scheler and Jaspers.[28] Moix, whose book is thorough and detailed, if often overly elegiac and uncritical, presumably drew
this information from Mounier's own chapter "Engagement"
in *Le Personnalisme* (a volume written in 1949 for the popular
collection "Que sais-je?"). Mounier writes, "This theme of
engagement, which goes back in any case to Scheler and to
Jaspers, had been circulated in France by *Esprit* before 1939,
before being taken up by existentialism in 1945, then
exploited to the point of abuse."[29] Three distinct claims are
made here, which bear brief investigation. Let us first examine the alleged German sources for the concept of engagement,[30] and then turn to the question of Mounier's priority in
France.

The first source named by Mounier is Max Scheler (1874-
1928). Scheler has been described as a Catholic phenome-
nological philosopher and as a Catholic personalist,[31] and is
perhaps best known for his treatment of the concept of *Ressentiment*. He is viewed by his admirers as one of the three founders of contemporary European philosophy, along with Husserl and Heidegger.[32] During the summer of 1924, Scheler
went to France and lectured at the "Entretiens d'Eté" in Pon-
tigny. These sessions, held in a former monastery and organized by Paul Desjardins, were attended by the intellectual elite
of Europe and were a very important mode of cultural exchange during the interwar years. Scheler is reported to have
caused quite a sensation with his lectures (in German) "on the
contemporary significance of St. Augustine and Meister Eck-

hardt, introducing his phenomenology and metaphysics in France at the same time."[33] His *Wesen und Formen der Sympathie* was published in French translation in 1928; however, the more famous *l'Homme du Ressentiment* did not appear until 1933.[34] Thus, there is some possibility that Scheler could have influenced his French colleagues before 1932.

However, neither Scheler nor his biographers claim that there is a concept in his philosophy which relates to engagement. Two striking pieces of evidence, which seem to prove definitively that Mounier's first claim was an error or a lapse of memory, deserve special mention here.

From 1928 to 1930, Georges Gurvitch, who was to become one of France's most distinguished sociologists, gave a series of lectures at the Sorbonne. These were aimed at introducing the new German philosophy to a French audience, and were published in book form in 1930, under the title *Les Tendances actuelles de la philosophie allemande*. Lectures on Husserl, Heidegger, and Scheler (the latter being defined as a "hierarchical personalist")[35] were included, though none on Jaspers. There is *not one* use of the word "engagement" in Gurvitch's book, whether in reference to Scheler or to any of the other philosophers under discussion.

Even more significant is the fact that as late as 1937, when P.-L. Landsberg, a priest and a member of the *Esprit* group, published a study of Scheler's philosophy, the word engagement is never used.[36] Yet in November of the same year, it was the same Landsberg who published "Réflexions sur l'engagement personnel," the first detailed, focused analysis of the concept to appear in *Esprit*.[37] We must conclude that while Scheler's writings may have aided Mounier and his collaborators in developing the French variant of personalism, there is no linkage between Scheler and engagement.

The same conclusion emerges from an examination of the possible influence of Karl Jaspers, the second source named by Mounier. For Jaspers (1883-1969), the decade of the 1920s was a time of almost total silence, in preparation for the publication of the important *Die geistige Situation der Zeit* in December 1931 (not translated into French until 1951). Then in 1932 appeared the three volumes of Jaspers' major opus, *Philosophie*. Therefore, only two of Jaspers' works could have been known in France by 1932. The first is *Allgemeine Psychopathologie*, a massive compendium fundamentally concerned with abnormal behavior (it will be remembered that Jaspers was originally trained as a physician). In this work, first published in 1913 and translated into French in 1928, Jaspers presents a complete survey of psychopathological theories, problems, and methods of cure. The second work, *Psychologie der Weltanschauungen* (1919) was never translated.[38]

It does seem probable that the philosophical renaissance in Germany in the 1920s was influential in creating an intellectual climate in France receptive to the concept of engagement. However, what is crucial for our purposes is that these German philosophers never used the term "engagement" in their writings. "Engagement" has no precise German equivalent, and later German authors, like the Americans, the English, and the Dutch, have borrowed the term from the French.[39]

While the Germans in the 1920s were deeply concerned with personal responsibility, it was the French who made the transition to political and social responsibility. But which Frenchmen, and when? In an excellent article on the "Rolland-Barbusse Debate," David James Fisher shows conclusively that the issues surrounding engagement were quite clearly understood by Romain Rolland as early as 1921. The whole question of the necessity of political involvement of intellectuals was intensively and systematically discussed in this fascinating public exchange of correspondence.[40]

Rolland even uses the verb form *engager* four times in this correspondence. In his second letter to Barbusse (February 2, 1922), Rolland indicates that he will cooperate with Barbusse and the communists. He admires their faith and their valor, but asks not to be obliged to share all their beliefs. This would be an "intolerable demand" and a political error, since some intellectuals feel a necessity to concern themselves with what the communists appear to overlook in their concern with everyday humanity. These intellectuals are still interested in "eternal humanity" (*l'humanité de toujours*).[41] Do you believe, Rolland continues, that "the contemporary duty of the artist, of the scholar, of the man of thought, is to engage himself, as in 1914 in the Army of Justice, in 1922 in the Army of the Revolution?"[42] (The French reads, *Croyez-vous que le devoir actuel de l'artiste, du savant, de l'homme de pensée, soit de s'engager, comme en 1914 dans l'Armée du Droit, en 1922 dans celle de la Révolution?*) This is a fascinating rejoinder, which shows that Rolland was far more sophisticated politically than has often been thought. He is reminding Barbusse, who had served in the First World War, that he, Rolland, had gone to Switzerland rather than join the "Army of Justice." Rolland's antiwar stance was of course vilified in 1914, but was honored by many, including Barbusse and the communists, in the immediate postwar years. Rolland is using *engager* in one of its traditional senses here, that of enlisting in the army, and although he is close, neither in this letter nor in the rest of his correspondence with Barbusse does he employ the term directly in a political meaning.[43]

Common usage of the noun "engagement" in its special contemporary political sense seems to have begun ten years after the Rolland-Barbusse debate. As late as February 1931, the well-known critic Albert Thibaudet used the phrase *écrivains de combat* to portray the type of involved writers who in a few years would be characterized as *écrivains engagés*.[44] At the same time it is indicative of how rapidly the concept of engagement spread in France that an established writer like André Gide could use the word in a letter to the *Association des Ecrivains et Artistes Révolutionnaires*, replying to a request that he join. The letter, dated December 13, 1932, begins: "No. The clearest result of such an engagement would be to prevent me immediately from writing anything more." Gide adds that he has already declared his strong support for the USSR but that he will be most helpful if he supplies his aid freely, "and if it is known that I am not enrolled."[45] (Interestingly enough, when Gide's writings from the 1930-1938 period were selected and published with an introduction by Yvonne Davet, the title chosen was *Littérature engagée*.)[46]

If we narrow our focus to 1932, we discover that Paul Nizan was using the term "engagement" in a fully contemporary sense in April of that year, several months before the first issue of Mounier's periodical *Esprit* appeared.[47] While an enterprising researcher may discover an earlier source (as William Johnston has done for *intellectuel*),[48] it seems fairly definite that "engagement" did not enter common French usage in its new sense until 1932. In any case, most intellectual historians would agree that the question of exact priorities is not as significant as when a term or a concept became popular. The rapid diffusion and widespread adoption of new ideas, of new ways of perceiving the world, often seem to occur in response to a particular historical situation, perhaps a crisis situation.

The year 1932 was an especially critical one for France, one of "cruel reawakening," after the "years of illusion" in the late 1920s. It was a more traumatic year for the French economy than 1929-1931, since the effects of the Depression were felt later in France. In fact, 1930 was the best year for the country's economy until 1950.[49] By 1932 the awareness of political crisis grew sufficiently for the parties of the Left to abandon some of their bitter infighting and take the initial steps in the formation of the Popular Front.[50] The situation in foreign affairs was of course very threatening, and 1933 was only a month old when Hitler came to power across the Rhine. François Goguel in his well-known study of political conflict in the Third Republic also picks 1932 as a critical year. The turning point Goguel selects is the fall of the Herriot cabinet in December 1932, which marked the smashing of all hope for European reconciliation and peaceful settlement of differences—hope that had risen out of the Locarno Treaties and Germany's entry into the League of Nations.[51]

It also seems fitting that as far as individuals are concerned, Paul Nizan—a ferocious critic of the abstaining, ivory-tower, "neutral" scholar—appears to have priority in the systematic use of "engagement." His biographer Ariel Ginsbourg describes him as a man who, "from adolescence on, found in political engagement his raison d'être."[52] According to his friend Jean-Albert Bédé, Nizan "could subsist only for engagement and through engagement."[53]

In *Les Chiens de garde*, first published in 1932, Nizan speaks of the rising sense of tension that is finally penetrating the comforting screen of self-deception erected by most intellectuals. By the early 1930s they were becoming aware of the menace that weighed over them. But, Nizan claims, these bourgeois intellectuals will never react with a "real engagement"—they will only aim at ideas.[54] Later he asserts that these same intellectuals will make "vague engagements" which become the basis of "bourgeois propaganda."[55] Nizan also uses the verb form *engager* five times in *Les Chiens de garde*, including twice on the same page in a denunciation of one of his favorite targets, the wealthy and influential academic philosopher Léon Brunschvicg.[56] At this time Nizan was calling for a "radical refusal" and full party commitment. Joining the French Communist Party is clearly what he meant in 1932 by "true" engagement.

Thus Nizan used the term "engagement" before Emmanuel Mounier, but did not pursue its implications much further, presumably because of his militancy within the Communist Party, the immense volume of his day-to-day journalism, and his parallel career as a novelist. In his second novel, *Le Cheval de Troie* (1935), and occasionally in his political journalism,[57] he did elaborate somewhat on engagement. *Le Cheval de Troie* is a fascinating account of the beginnings of social disruption during the 1930s in a small French town, and by extension to much of France. A fascist meeting is scheduled in a community that had known no wars, no invasions for centuries. Now there is violence; no longer are the French an "incorruptible *petit monde*." "The historical explosion," which had seemed "a dream and a legend that did not any longer concern the sleepy and distracted French provinces," had finally come. It carried with it "that reality, that heaviness of engagements, which include death."[58] Nizan's heroes are communist militants, and they are planning a counter-manifestation. He writes, "there are actions which engage nothing but changes of habit, of language." These are not serious, he asserts editorially. Those which count are those that include the risk of death before attaining one's goal. "One changes nothing without risking death." These men and women are "engaging their lives."[59]

TOWARD A DEFINITION OF ENGAGEMENT— MOUNIER'S CONTRIBUTION

Perhaps the Catholic Emmanuel Mounier never gave credit to the militant anti-Catholic Paul Nizan for the latter's prior use of the concept of engagement because there were more similarities between the two men, even in mode of argument and intellectual approach, than either would have ever admitted. Both were born in the French provinces in 1905, Mounier in Grenoble, Nizan in Tours. Both were *agrégés* in philosophy, both abandoned the teaching profession for more active and public careers. The two men traded insults and accusations during the early 1930s, and seem to have had a fairly intense dislike for each other. Nizan was persuaded that the *Esprit* group would turn fascist,[60] and Mounier took delight in frequently criticizing Nizan's militant communism in the pages of *Esprit*, and also reminded Nizan of a fact that must have been deeply embarrassing to him—his brief period of youthful involvement in the *Action Française*.[61]

If Mounier does not have precedence over Nizan, it is undeniable that he and his group devoted the most attention during the 1930s to clarifying and defining engagement. The group of brilliant young intellectuals which gathered around Mounier and *Esprit* comprise the most important and interesting of the "nonconformist" youth movements which shared a "will to renewal," disgust and dismay at the current political and economic situation of France and Europe, and a desire to transcend the normal left-right distinctions of France's traditional political parties. These movements were all founded between 1930 and 1933 and have been well documented by Jean-Louis Loubet del Bayle.[62] Of these movements the *Esprit* group was the only one to survive to maturity. If we wish to persist with the question, "What was Engagement?" we must turn to the pages of *Esprit*.

In the early issues of *Esprit*, beginning with No. 1, October 1932, there is extensive discussion of social and political action, especially in the famous "Refaire la Renaissance," drafted by Mounier himself. In this long manifesto Mounier analyzes both the necessity for, and the dangers of, action for the Christian. Among the dangers mentioned are becoming trapped by formulas, presumably like the Marxists, and placing too much emphasis on the "I," so that one becomes a self-satisfied, sanctimonious "do-gooder." These are the difficulties, Mounier writes, for those of us "who engage ourselves."[63] With Julien Benda obviously in mind, he adds, "It is necessary to be done with the betrayals (*trahisons*) of action, as with the betrayals of thought." Mounier later added, "A secret circulates among Christians: that of their *trahisons*."[64]

Another problem which will reemerge in many later discussions of engagement is delineated by Mounier in his October 1932 call to action. He stresses that "our action is not essentially directed toward success, but toward bearing witness (*témoignage*)."[65] This point is clarified and modified somewhat in a rebuttal to criticisms from two fellow Catholics, Robert Garric and François Mauriac. Writing in the May 1933 issue of *Esprit*, Mounier asserts that it is not possible to accept various necessities before deciding to act.[66] In other words, "wiser" heads were urging him to calm down and be realistic about possibilities for success before entering the arena. Mounier's teacher, Jacques Chevalier, made the same criticism of his pupil in a memorial note written in 1950, regretting the way Mounier had evolved. His action began too soon: "This engagement, in my judgment premature, . . . occurred before the instrument, that is to say himself, was completely ready." As a consequence Mounier exhausted his forces while still young, and exaggerated faults that he,

Chevalier, had combatted in his young student.[67] It is clear that Chevalier, who remained to the right of Mounier politically, in fact serving as Minister of Education during the Vichy regime, is saying that engagement may be justified in some circumstances, but only when one is physically and intellectually mature. In this case, and perhaps quite often as professors watch their favorite students evolve in directions they disapprove, what is meant is that engagement should have been postponed until the pupil thought like the master.

However, Mounier would have none of such cautions. Instead, predating the Sartre of *What is Literature?* by some twelve years,[68] Mounier states: "As if the first act of this adhesion to the call of mankind was not the refusal of all that is [i.e., the world of political realities] because being (*l'être*) is infinitely more and infinitely other than that which is." It is true, Mounier adds, that "facts are our masters, but it is still more true that the vocation of mankind is to create facts."[69]

In the same (May 1933) article Mounier stresses that action for the involved Christian demands an absolute commitment. (Nizan, as we have seen, made an identical demand, but from very different premises.) Mounier writes, "the absolute is that which engages every minute and engages it infinitely beyond itself." Again quite close to the Nizan of *Les Chiens de garde*,[70] Mounier challenges pure intellect. Intelligence has value only through "the object it works upon." If one is dealing with techniques and systems, one can do a job, but ". . . it is not worth our lives. The Spirit (*L'Esprit*) is an engagement, and one engages himself with all his soul and all his days before him. Our labor of revolutionary criticism is a position taken against injustice before being an effort to construct justice." From the vantage point of mid-1933, Mounier is certain that a revolution is in the offing, and indeed hopes one will come. "It is our profound spiritual exigency." If the result is failure, his group will nonetheless have borne witness. *Témoigner* is used again: "A life that has sustained a great *témoignage* is not broken. . . . We know our weaknesses, and we also know the grandeur of our *témoignage*."[71]

Thus by May 1933, Emmanuel Mounier has gone on clear

public record as having a definition of engagement and some awareness of the problems and contradictions it posed. Mounier does not specifically indicate that he was aware of the original meaning of *témoignage*, which was equated with martyrdom, bearing witness for Christ.[72] Later, however, he did perceive the difficulty that emerges if one links engagement too closely with *témoignage*. In dealing with engagement in his 1949 book on Personalism, Mounier stresses that to be viable one's action must have both a will to be efficacious and a spiritual ingredient. It is a double polarity, prophetic and political, and a constant tension between the two poles must exist.[73] If one remains a pure philosopher and awaits a perfect cause one will never act. "The Absolute is not of this world and is not commensurable with this world. We never engage ourselves save in debatable combats for imperfect causes. Yet to refuse engagement for this reason is to refuse the human condition."[74]

During the 1930s Mounier tried to live up to his high principles, "to take sides without being a party man" (*prendre parti sans être l'homme d'un parti*).[75] *Esprit* continued to pursue an independent and rather courageous line, risking at least once but in the end escaping Papal condemnation, and taking on many of the sacred cows of French bourgeois society—*travail, argent, patrie*, for example. Issues were also devoted to education, the economy, the viability of dialogue with the socialists, and an attack on "fascist pseudovalues." With issue No. 16 (January 1934), the format of the periodical was changed and a brief statement inserted at the beginning of each issue, entitled "Our Positions." The reader is informed that *Esprit* had been founded two years previously by a group of young men who were determined to liquidate the failures of the modern world and realize a new order based primarily on spiritual values. Their goal was to "undo [or untie—the French is *délier*] these values [i.e., the spiritual ones] from their compromises with the established disorder; engage them in revolutions which *they* will command" (my italics).

This very interesting if somewhat confusing formula was

included at the head of each issue through April 1934; in May the editors changed "Our Positions" to brief statements on a different subject each month, rather than one summary of their doctrine. The passage cited above does seem to say that values must always be predominant; in fact the Christian enters the world of action by engaging his or her values. The kinds of problems that Mounier hinted at as early as the first issue of *Esprit* appear to have resurfaced with "Our Positions." Mounier and the personalists around him seem to have broken the tension between pure political involvement and irresponsible martyristic *témoignage*, in favor of the latter.[76]

If we tentatively accept the definition we have been deriving from Mounier, it is clear that true engagement can be neither the *témoignage* of the Christian martyr, nor the violent action of that archetypal figure in twentieth-century fact and fiction known usually as the "adventurer." The adventurer may also be a brilliant intellectual, but he cannot be truly engaged, as Roger Stéphane points out in his illuminating study, *Portrait de l'aventurier*, first published in 1950 with a preface by Jean-Paul Sartre. Stéphane studied three famous adventurers—T. E. Lawrence, André Malraux, and Ernst von Salomon—men who tried to change themselves by or through action, who demanded justification for their acts, who tried to find a kind of salvation through facing danger. Such a man, writes Sartre in his preface, may join a revolutionary party during a war or crisis, but ". . . he remains suspect in the eyes of his allies, and he does not love them."[77] This is not surprising, since he was not forced to fight. These adventurers, who are also sometimes termed heroes or terrorists, are "the parasites of the militants." (A militant is one who, following Mounier's dichotomy between prophetic and political polarities, has broken the tension on the side of politics.) The militant comes into the communist party, or any other party which demands a total commitment from its members, not for personal reasons, not in an effort to resolve internal moral conflicts. He even takes his wife from within the party. Sartre characterizes the militant as an individual with no depth, no secrets, no complexes, no private life.

The adventurer, on the other hand, knows that if the militants he collaborates with in the revolutionary parties are victorious, he will be rejected immediately; therefore he is constantly tempted by suicide, and knows that he is going to die for nothing. According to Sartre the adventurer is *"engagé* in action to escape solitude, yet he finds himself more alone than ever."[78] In his analysis of the three adventurer-intellectuals, Roger Stéphane points out a striking coincidence. "As if to underline the fragility of their engagement," each of the three writers in their literary work "describes at length a confrontation with a traitor."[79] The engagement of the adventurer is therefore tenuous, and best given another name; "existential gambling" is the term I would prefer to use, even though the adventurer appears to be making a total commitment and has no compunctions about risking his life. These distinctions, if persuasive, would oblige us to reexamine some of our common assumptions about André Malraux, who has been popularly viewed as "the archetypal *homme engagé*, the intellectual man of action."[80]

If we continue to follow the guidelines set down by Emmanuel Mounier, it would seem equally inappropriate to apply the term engagement to the actions of the typical "militant" as described above, whether he or she is a communist or a member of some other rigorously organized party. The relationship between engagement and membership in a communist party will be discussed in more detail in Chapter III, and in Chapter IV fascist engagement will be examined. It will become apparent that there are no easy answers, and that Mounier's categories may be too rigid. At this point, however, we must emphasize that according to the principal early theorist of engagement, one cannot be a communist or a fascist and be truly *engagé*. Why this is true is subtly illustrated in Louis Bodin's work, *Les Intellectuels*. In his section dealing with intellectuals and communism, Bodin notes that over the years a substantial number of intellectuals joined the party for a period of time, and then broke away, spiteful, ". . . embittered from an engagement which came to seem an insupportable alienation."[81] For Mounier the kind of unquestioning party involvement Bodin is describing would be better categorized as fanaticism, or in the very useful terminology coined by P.-L. Landsberg in his landmark 1937 essay on engagement, *embrigadement*.[82] (It is impossible, I think, to translate *embrigadement* successfully into English. But the meaning of the word should be clear, given its military root.)

Bringing *embrigadement* into the discussion may, however, create more problems than it resolves, since it confronts us with the thorny, probably unresolvable, question of standards. One must recognize that what is true engagement for a given individual may be *embrigadement* for another, and would be seen by a third as folly, or even criminality. To take one brief example, it would be arguable that Paul Nizan himself was primarily *embrigadé* during the 1930s, and that only during the few months between his resignation from the French Communist Party in September 1939 and his death in May 1940 was he truly *engagé*. Someone like Louis Aragon, surely the most famous French intellectual who has remained steadfastly loyal to the Party, and who appears never to have forgiven his long-deceased friend for "deserting," would of course take the opposite position.

If we cannot hope to settle the matter of standards, we can note with more certainty that *some* distinction between pure political involvement and engagement is widely recognized. French intellectuals were not alone in this awareness, as Stuart Samuels points out in his valuable study of British intellectuals and politics in the 1930s. During the early period, 1926-1930, when the Auden group was in formation, the young Englishmen faced no moral dilemma, no choice between private art and political action. They could be romantic Marxists, Samuels writes, because ". . . the potential conflict, between political commitment and moral engagement, although recognized, had yet to raise its inconvenient head."[83]

A similar point is made by Emmanuel Mounier's biographer, Candide Moix, who argues that Mounier's political thought was the weakest element in his work.[84] When *Esprit* was founded, Mounier believed that there was a "possible accord between thought and political action," while admitting that there would always be a tension. *Esprit* was neither a political review nor a review of pure thought, ". . . but nonetheless an engagement. . . . And every engagement leads to contact with the impurities of action. Mounier suffered from this."[85] Moix's conclusion slightly contradicts this argument and suggests that he, like Mounier himself on occasion, has swung the balance too far away from the admittedly painful contact with the "impurities of action. . . ." He writes of Mounier, "*Engagé*, that he was, all his life, but within the particular format of intellectual engagement."[86]

Moix's intriguing formula does echo an implication which emerged from our discussion of the roots of engagement in the Dreyfus Affair, namely that there is a close, perhaps even symbiotic, relationship between engagement and intellectuals as a sub-class with a conscious sense of group identity. Whether the one can exist without the other will be discussed in Chapter v. In fairness, we must admit that linking intellectuals and engagement conflicts with the operational definition of "intellectual" employed by most academic sociologists. For example, Talcott Parsons defines the intellectual as one who devotes himself to cultural considerations "over and above . . . societal commitments." Parsons also defines intellectuals in terms of what they are not—e.g., primary holders of political power and of economic resources.[87]

Whether or not intellectuals can exist apart from engagement, it is clear that to have engagement there must be intellectuals. It does now seem possible to propose a definition which is faithful to the intent of Mounier and his colleagues in the 1930s who first analyzed engagement. The most useful definition of engagement would disallow *témoignage, embrigadement*, and "existential gambling," the violent commitment of the adventurer-intellectual. It is assumed that the individuals involved will have a clear awareness of their identity as intellectuals, and that in some fashion their action will be group oriented. With these clarifications we may define engagement as the political or social action of an intellectual who has realized that abstention is a ruse, a commitment to the *status quo*, and who makes a conscious and willful choice to enter the arena, never abandoning his or her critical judgment.[88]

Even though this definition might be applicable in an ideal type sense to all times and places, if we find it acceptable we may conclude that engagement is a phenomenon best understood historically. Only with the Dreyfus Affair did intellectuals develop a fully articulated sense of being a separate group within society.[89] As far as the present is concerned, a persuasive case can be made that the specific factors which tended to elicit engagement have either disappeared from or are no longer operative in contemporary technological society. On the other hand, if J. P. Nettl is correct, and if the true intellectual (as opposed to the mandarin) is impelled toward engagement by the very nature of the work he or she does,[90] then we may expect occasional manifestations of engagement in the future.

II

◊◊◊◊◊◊◊◊◊

The Case against Engagement:
Julien Benda and
La Trahison des Clercs

◊◊◊◊◊◊◊◊◊

Once again, where are the traitors?

Raymond Aron[1]

Could we, the social scientists, have somehow betrayed ourselves during the past couple of decades by
what is false within? Has there been anything re-
sembling what Julien Benda called a *trahison des clercs*?

Robert A. Nisbet[2]

WHO BETRAYED?

The idea of a treason or betrayal of the intellectuals has had an
enormous success. This concept may be viewed as the reverse
of the coin of engagement, or perhaps a slightly distorted
mirror-image. It has become a commonplace in America and
England. In France it may be traced back at least to the
Dreyfus Affair, when intellectuals acquired along with their
name a special critical function, and because of the victory
signified by the revision of Dreyfus' first trial, gained "a *droit
de cité* unknown in other countries."[3] Both Dreyfusard and
anti-Dreyfusard intellectuals accused each other of betraying
their "true" functions.[4] The explicit formulation of *La Trahison des clercs* did not, however, come until 1927, and in France
at least the concept has become inseparably (and rightfully)
identified with Julien Benda.

Though he has had a number of distinguished American admirers over the years, including T. S. Eliot,[5] Julien Benda is not well known in this country. Specialists in French literature and intellectual history will recognize him as a polemicist and critic, a second-rank figure who throughout his very long life (1867-1956) was overshadowed by several generations of brilliant contemporaries. He is remembered primarily for one book, though he wrote fifty and more than one thousand articles. *La Trahison des clercs* was first published in 1927, and translated into English in 1928 as *The Treason of the Intellectuals*.

Benda's controversial attack on *certain types*[6] of modern intellectuals has often been dismissed as unscholarly polemic. In his introduction to *The New Radicalism in America, 1889-1963*, Christopher Lasch states: ". . . I have not wished to write a tract, another *Trahison des clercs*, and I state my own prejudices here only in order to make it clear what they are, not because this book is intended to document them."[7]

Even when Benda's contribution has been viewed positively, it has been rather badly misperceived. In April 1965 a symposium on "The Intellectual in Politics" was held at the University of Texas, and the proceedings were published in 1966 with a preface by H. Malcolm Macdonald. Macdonald felt that despite the divergencies of the views of the participants, a consensus did emerge, ". . . on the necessity of the intellectual, however defined, to remain true to his task of being what Julien Benda has called 'the conscience of humanity.' "[8] In a vague and general sense that every intellectual from Ayn Rand to Herbert Marcuse could probably accept, Macdonald's assertion is correct. However, a close reading of the eight papers presented at the symposium reveals an almost total ignorance of the specifics of Benda's thought. Only one speaker, the Swedish political scientist and parliamentarian Gunnar Hecksher, refers specifically to *La Trahison des clercs*, but his brief remarks show little understanding of what Benda was advocating in that work.[9] One other participant, the

German historian Klaus Mehnert, does take a position close to that adopted by Benda in *La Trahison des clercs*, but he never mentions Benda by name.[10]

Eugene McCarthy, at the time Senator from Wisconsin, was the last speaker at the symposium, and McCarthy made an eloquent plea for greater political involvement on the part of intellectuals. Without reference to Julien Benda, Senator McCarthy used the phrase "treason of the intellectuals" in *exactly* the opposite sense originally intended by Benda.[11] No one would accuse Senator McCarthy, a man deeply steeped in Catholic theology and a talented poet and essayist in his own right, of lacking intellectual credentials. It is interesting to recall that two years after this speech was delivered McCarthy became the leader of the "Dump Johnson" movement, which attracted many American intellectuals and which appears to be a rare case of intellectuals having some demonstrable political influence, in that President Lyndon Johnson did not seek a second full term of office in 1968.[12]

Senator McCarthy's "error" does suggest that while the notion of the "treason of the intellectuals" is very much a part of our political climate, there is no widespread awareness of the authorship of the term. Even when Benda's authorship is recognized, the precise meanings he attached to the concept of *la trahison des clercs* have long been forgotten, and there has been heated debate, since the Second World War at least, as to precisely what segment of the intellectual class is treasonous. One's own political predispositions clearly play a major role in determining whom one identifies as the betrayers.

To deal fully with the uses and misuses of Benda's concept of the betrayal of the intellectuals would require a long essay. As an illustration of the diversity of views, here are four examples chosen from a large number.

> Lawrence Stone defines the "ultimate *trahison des clercs*" as "the conscious denigration of the life of the mind."[13]

> Robert Brustein says "We have been witnessing a modern *trahison des clercs*, signified by the surrender of men

and women with great potential to America's hunger for personalities."[14]

Ferdinand Mount defines the treason of the clerks as "this prostration of mind before brutish might, not excluding that of Julien Benda, who coined the phrase. . . ."[15]

Richard Cobb defines the *trahison des clercs* as "intellectual commitment to political extremism."[16]

A MAN WHO DETESTED CHAPELS

The controversy over *la trahison des clercs* continues and Benda remains relatively obscure. One reason for this apparent paradox is suggested by René Etiemble in his preface to the third edition of *La Trahison des clercs* (1958). Etiemble points out that for more than half a century Benda had obstinately refused every philosophical and political "mode." Benda produced polemics against Bergsonian intuition, Maurrassian sophism, and later intellectual "fads" such as surrealism and existentialism. Throughout his long life he had never received much except "hatred and sarcasm," had never reached many people, and had gained several thousand influential enemies with one work. *La Trahison des clercs* infuriated the literary people, who are especially "rancorous and vain." The media, Etiemble adds, which in a few weeks can make an "inoffensive imbecile" into a star, spent fifty years lowering Julien Benda into the image of a "fanatical, odious, and raging little man."[17] Julien Benda was, as André Lwoff writes, a nonconformist, a man who "detested chapels."[18] When he died in extreme old age his passing was barely noticed.[19]

While Benda's technical mastery of French literary style has never been questioned, his methods of argumentation may also help to explain his lack of eminence. Readers who are familiar with *La Trahison des clercs*, even those in sympathy with Benda's fundamental positions, may well conclude that the imprecise knowledge of what Benda stood for is deserved. Raymond Aron, author of another, very different polemic against a large group of his fellow intellectuals, finds Benda's arguments often confused. Aron writes: ". . . if the betrayal consists in overvaluing the temporal and undervaluing the eternal, the intellectuals of our time are all traitors."[20]

While Aron's formulation is persuasive, it is not a completely correct definition of what Benda came to view the betrayal to be. Benda would have been in full accord with Aron's assertion that ". . . the tendency to criticize the established order is, so to speak, the occupational disease of the intellectuals."[21] Yet the matter is complicated because Benda would by no means claim that the criterion for discerning betrayal is criticism of the established order. In many cases it would be a betrayal *not* to challenge, and challenge publicly, the established order.

Pierre Chambat has shown, through a close examination of Benda's entire opus, that Benda was concerned with what he perceived as a "crisis of civilization."[22] Even in *La Trahison des clercs*, Benda did not limit himself to the rather specific question of "Who betrayed?" He attempted to deal with many, if not all, facets of the intellectual's role in modern society. Such inquiries inevitably pose serious difficulties, since the individual commitment of the writer is so deeply enmeshed in the problem he is studying. Robert J. Niess, author of the definitive published biography of Julien Benda, recognizes these difficulties and proposes an interesting, if somewhat discouraging solution: "To discover the true role of the *clerc*, to learn whether or not he has betrayed, and to date the betrayal successfully would be the task of the perfect historian, that is, the unfalteringly alert mind, not only universally learned but completely impartial both politically and intellectually and strengthened by the most rigorous kind of philosophical training."[23] Niess believes that Benda was especially weak as an historian.[24] While Niess' judgment of Benda's skill as an historian may be disputed,[25] his own analysis of the origins of *La Trahison des clercs* has been recognized as a masterful exercise in the history of ideas.[26] The concept of the *clerc* is traced by Niess back to *Dialogue à Byzance*, published in 1900. Already Benda conceived of a body of *clercs* serving as the conscience of society, but it took him a long time to develop his central idea of a mass treason of the intellectuals.[27] *La Trahison des clercs* is viewed as the essential document in Benda's intellectual life; at least with the hindsight we now possess he seems to have been progressing toward it all through his early and middle career, and after 1927 he constantly amplifies and defends it.

Niess' own judgment of *La Trahison des clercs* is quite ambivalent. There is a rather striking dichotomy between high praise and sharp criticism, which suggests that he was uncertain in his own evaluation. Niess points up many of the vagaries and inconsistencies in Benda's argumentation, the flagrant biases, and even finds examples of faulty reasoning. Yet he is convinced that in the future *La Trahison des clercs* will be seen as the one work which best combines Benda's passion and logic into a "brilliant system of social criticism."[28] Niess is persuaded that it will hold up as "one of the most considerable books of our time."[29] This dichotomy is again manifested in Niess' conclusions on Benda's entire career. He is quite severe; Benda made a "catastrophic intellectual error, the error of constant generalization without sufficient regard to facts. . . ." Yet Benda will someday be conceded an "honorable place in that brilliant line which he himself described, the line of St. Paul and Luther and Pascal, men who eternally prevent the world from slumbering in indolence and evil."[30]

It seems unlikely that Benda will acquire this prominence (since he never had it during his lifetime) and retain it simply because he made people angry and kept them alert. Perhaps Niess felt that intellectuals reading Benda would sense intuitively that his message was an important one, reminding them of truths about their calling. H. Stuart Hughes, in his pathbreaking study of the intellectual history of Europe between 1890 and 1930, *Consciousness and Society*, selects *La Trahison des clercs* as one of three works of "intellectual summation," a "directional signpost" for the middle and late 1920s.[31] On balance Hughes is even more critical than Niess, and he finds *La Trahison des clercs* a deeply flawed book. Hughes does, however, value the work as a "moral remonstrance," and a call to an "examination of conscience."[32]

What is the nature of this "moral remonstrance" that both Niess and Hughes find in *La Trahison des clercs*? For Hughes it must be an important factor, since without it Benda's simplification of the issues, his "profoundly parochial outlook," his "narrowness of intellectual range," would hardly make the book worthy of mention.[33]

THE ORIGINAL CONCEPTION OF
LA TRAHISON DES CLERCS

Julien Benda never pretended to be a tolerant man; he hated his ideological and political enemies with an unremitting passion. Many readers will be annoyed by his stubborn refusal to consider opposing views, his digressions, his merciless hammering at the same points. Still the central line of his argument in *La Trahison des clercs* can be disentangled. A careful reformulation of this argument should serve three purposes. First, in viewing the strengths and weaknesses of the work in clearer focus, the reader will be able to evaluate its importance for himself or herself. Second, Benda's intellectual and political evolution after 1927 will be easier to comprehend, in particular the quite fascinating and apparently contradictory changes in his views on the political involvement of intellectuals. The common misconception of Benda as purely an "ivory-tower" theorist will be laid to rest definitively. I also hope to show that even in 1927 the question of political action of the *clerc*, and thus the question of engagement, posed the crucial paradox for Benda. Benda may have resolved it to his own satisfaction, though I doubt even that and find his ambivalence showing through in the very vehemence of his denials. The other ambivalence—that of the commentators—has, I believe, its roots in the same paradox. Benda touches painful nerves and reflects, in his own way, the doubts and hesitations felt by several generations of practicing intellectuals in Europe and America.

Benda opens *La Trahison des clercs* by formulating the essential qualities he finds in modern society at large. Both the intellectuals and humanity in general have been placing greater and greater emphasis on temporal concerns. This is an age of politics; political passions and those of race and class are now reaching almost everybody, even spreading to the Far East.[34] (Benda may have been thinking of the Chinese Revolution of 1927, though as is almost always the case he makes no specific historical reference. He prefers to remain on a general, theoretical plane.) We know, Benda adds, precisely who our political enemies are, and thus we can hate them more bitterly. A "condensation" of political hatreds has developed, along with a greater uniformity of thought.[35]

Again and again Benda stresses the growth of nationalist passion, the overweening concern with national glory and pride. He is horrified by new doctrines which advocate crushing enemy cultures totally, rather than incorporating the vanquished within the conquering society. Benda's distress at the rise of mystical nationalism cannot be overemphasized, and he frequently returns to the subject throughout his work. He devotes almost as much attention to the related issue of the rise of ideology in general. The passions of the past were precisely passions—that is, "naive explosions of instinct,"[36] with no theoretical grounding. However, a broad spectrum of intellectuals, from Karl Marx to Charles Maurras and their varied followers, have elaborated networks of doctrines designed to support political passions. These networks are effective and have increased the strength of political passions.[37] Buttressed by a careful intellectual organization, each of the modern ideological systems argues that it is the "agent of good" in the world, and that its enemy represents the "genie of evil." Each system tries to be totalitarian, in the sense of covering all aspects of life, believing itself destined to succeed, and claiming that its ideology is founded on science.[38]

Benda believes that these new, systematized passions arise from two fundamental desires: (1) temporal good, and (2) the wish to be separate and unique from other human groups. The former relates to class passion, the latter to racial passion, and nationalism unites the two. These passions are realist in that they relate to the world and are nonidealist, though they are so strong that one might term them "divinized realism."[39] Men want to be in the real and practical world and not in the disinterested, metaphysical realm; no one would die now for "principles," for abstract universal values like justice. Older idealist passions, such as those motivating a "pure" crusader, have been absorbed by nationalism. The pragmatic behavior of a single localized state has become divinized—the state has become God and Mussolini's Italy admits it.[40] Later in *La Trahison des clercs* Benda comments with disgust on the Italian intellectuals' eulogy of warfare and scorn for civilian life, their praise of the morality of violence. He finds their apologies for the warlike instinct a "stupefaction of history."[41]

The reader with some general knowledge of Benda's positions may be confused at this point, for he descends from the ivory tower into the heat of a polemic against a specific regime, even before he has elaborated his doctrine of the role of the *clerc*. Over the years his attacks on Italian fascism grew more vehement, especially after the invasion of Ethiopia.[42]

Perhaps Benda realized that his remarks on Italy could lead him into a logical dilemma, for he makes the qualification that the *clerc* may become involved in external politics when an abstract injustice has been committed. (Of course, he can provide us with no universally applicable key to determine when an event may be classified as a true injustice, though he names Voltaire's role in the Calas Affair, and Zola's advocacy of Dreyfus' innocence as examples of justified involvement.) He could have cited his own participation in the Dreyfus Affair, which Pierre Chambat, in his judicious analysis of this aspect of Benda's career, does not hesitate to term "engagement."[43] Only a decade later, in 1936, did Benda publicly admit and discuss his involvement in the Dreyfus Affair. This led Paul Nizan to remark that Benda "wanted to see in the Affair only a combat of eternal verities, when, in fact, it was simply a matter of an historical engagement."[44]

Enough examples have been given to show that when Benda mentions specifics, it is easy to detect a leftist, or at least a liberal political inclination. I shall return to this important point later. Presumably Benda felt himself on surer ground in *La Trahison des clercs* when he added two *general* criteria for involvement. First, the true *clerc* never espouses causes for any personal gain. Also, if the *clerc* is really fulfilling his function he will be scorned and insulted by the layman.[45]

Here, then, is the first mention of the problem of when and why the intellectual should enter the political arena. Benda's embarrassment is, I believe, evident to the reader. Probably because it is more difficult to prescribe contemporary behavior than to look to the past with the benefit of present knowledge, Benda devotes more attention in *La Trahison des clercs* to the question of how the intellectuals should have responded to the recent and dramatic changes in that part of humanity which he terms "lay" as opposed to clerical.

In the past the *clercs* had stood apart from the masses, were devoted to the metaphysical and the speculative, and scorned practical ends. This elite boasted a lineage of two thousand years and had always been in ". . . formal opposition to the realism of the multitudes." Thanks to the vigilance of these intellectual sentinels, humanity had at least ". . . done evil while honoring the good."[46] This contradiction was the honor of humanity and kept civilization on its proper course until around 1890. At that time a sharp transition took place, and those who had been a "brake" on the realism of the masses began to stimulate that realism.[47] To show that there is a qualitative difference in the contemporary period Benda cites individuals—Theodor Mommsen, Heinrich von Treitschke, Ferdinand Brunetière, Maurice Barrès, Charles Maurras, Gabriele d'Annunzio, Rudyard Kipling, and his former friend Charles Péguy, who had died during the first

Battle of the Marne in 1914. The names of Georges Sorel and Friedrich Nietzsche are then added for good measure, and Benda finds everyone on the list to be equally evil. All are men of true political passion. (It is important to note that all of these intellectuals, with the possible exceptions of Péguy and Sorel, about whom there is heated scholarly debate,[48] are strongly identified with the political Right. Had he been so inclined, Benda could have included in his first list of betrayers prominent, indeed internationally known, intellectuals who were active in left-wing causes, such as Romain Rolland and Henri Barbusse. The latter had been a member of the French Communist Party since 1923.)

The group of intellectuals Benda chose to denounce are condemned because they desire action and immediate results and have descended eagerly into the political forum. No disinterested group remains; the modern *clerc* is strongly xenophobic.

Benda does admit that external historical circumstances have played some role in this change in clerical attitudes, though he still wishes that the *clercs* had not acquiesced so joyfully. The historians, as guilty as the novelists and poets, are glorifying nationalism, producing pragmatic rather than disinterested work, and using history to strengthen political causes. The literary critics are unobjective and partisan; even the metaphysicians, supposedly the most abstract of all, are becoming political. The latter change is, Benda claims, totally without historical precedent.[49]

"Intense" is a mild word to describe the degree of Benda's own French patriotism, and though he set forth an elaborate series of arguments to defend his loyalty to France,[50] he is susceptible to the charge of xenophobia himself. His indictment of Germany, "the cancer of Europe," began in 1905 and persisted through his last published articles in 1954.[51] As one might expect, he claims that the German philosophers, such as Fichte and Hegel, were the first to betray. Though the French have all too frequently heeded the siren song of their colleagues across the Rhine, "the nationalist *clerc* is essentially a German invention."[52] Instead of honoring the abstract quality of what is uniquely human, the nineteenth-century German intellectuals began the trend of looking concretely at mankind so that differences become clearly visible. Even Christianity, and the agnostic Benda was always an admirer of the early Christians, has been subverted by the nationalists. Christ has been made a "professor of national egotism."[53] Marxism in its guise as internationalist philosophy is not a valid substitute, Benda believes, since it has concrete aims and speaks in the name of one group, instead of all humanity.

The legacy of Hellenism, which for a time had been maintained by the classical French intellectuals, has at least been defeated. The modern *clerc* has the infantile wish to think of everything as "in time," never as outside or beyond time, and is concerned only with the contemporaneous, the immediate, present circumstances.[54] One can see how appalled Benda would have been at the emphasis on "relevance," which was so important in American university curricula in the 1960s. The powerful new trend toward pragmatic career training which has surfaced in American (and European) colleges and universities in the 1970s would have equally distressed him. Benda finds all such new doctrines a reversal of Platonism, since they claim that real values are seen and concrete instead of "clouds" (*nuées*) of justice and temperance.[55] For the first time in history *clercs* approve the judges of Socrates. Again and again Benda attacks the moral flavor the new *clercs* have given to realism, while stressing repeatedly that we are at a turning point in history. "The divinisation of the political" is the greatest and most evil work of the modern *clercs*.[56] Even Machiavelli said that politics and morality were disassociated, and Charles Maurras now claims that "politics determine morality."[57]

The new emphasis on man's natural violence especially distresses Benda, along with the preference for authoritarian regimes. When confronted with barbaric behavior, the *clercs* now invoke human nature and claim that nothing can be done. They have forgotten that the moralist is essentially a "utopian" and they derive a romantic pleasure from pessimism. The *clercs* even praise war for itself and not as a "sad necessity."[58] Modern man is turning to Sparta for inspiration. The *clercs* have created and popularized a new honor—the honor of practical courage leading to the conquest of things. In Benda's view civilization is simply not possible unless functions are divided, and they are no longer divided when the *clercs* are laicized. Thus the general anti-intellectualism, the exalting of the man of arms over the man of study, the praise of action over thought, the unconscious over intellect, are to be expected.

Benda is convinced that despite all the pressures to conform it is possible for individual *clercs* to resist and remain independent. He clearly believes as strongly as does Noam Chomsky in the responsibility of intellectuals.[59] If one is a real thinker, Benda states, he will be a universalist. However, today humanity wants its scholars to be "not guides but servants," and for the most part, that is what humanity gets.[60] The general conclusion of *La Trahison des clercs* is that the political realism of the *clercs* is not a random fact but instead "linked to the essence of the modern world."[61] The sceptic might accuse Benda of vast oversimplification and infer that he found the entire world to be treasonous, except himself, of course. Benda might have agreed with the second point, if pressed on the matter. He argues that because of the *clercs*' evasion of their duty, humanity now both perpetrates evil and honors it. Perhaps because of his deep-rooted pessimism, Benda was often an accurate prophet, and he predicts that civilization will move toward "the most total and perfect war that the world will have ever seen."[62] It should be emphasized that these words were written in the relative calm of the mid-1920s, several years before the sense of living in a period "between two wars" became prevalent.[63] Whether this new war is to be between nations or classes, Benda's diagnosis is somber. He sees little hope for peace and finds that most pacifist doctrines weaken the true cause of peace.[64]

Benda pulls all his arguments together in a final summary,

where he adopts a more inflexible position than he had earlier in the work. He now states that the true *clerc* must be *totally* disengaged from society. When the *clerc* declares to mankind that his "kingdom is not of this world," he may be crucified, ". . . but he is respected and his word haunts the memory of men."[65] Yet in the real world of 1927 the betrayers dominate—Nietzsche, Sorel, Barrès, and their ilk, and Benda emphasizes again that this is no temporary aberration but rather a permanent trend in world historical development.[66]

Benda wonders whether realism may not after all be the dominant force in human society. Coupled with the growing conquest of Nature, realism could easily produce a relapse into the worst forms of violence and cruelty—another striking prediction for 1933-1945. The best that one can hope for, Benda believes, is some form of union of nations and classes, though the "universal fraternity" which would emerge is not really desirable. It would merely be a higher form of nationalism, with the nation calling itself Man, and naming God as the enemy.

> And henceforth, unified into an immense army, into an immense factory, no longer aware of anything save heroism, discipline, inventions, scorning all free and disinterested activity, no longer placing the Good above the real world, and having for God only itself and its wishes, humanity will attain great things—that is, a really grandiose control over the matter which surrounds it, a really joyous consciousness of its power and its grandeur. And history will smile to think that Socrates and Jesus died for this species.[67]

LA TRAHISON DES CLERCS AFTER 1927

There are hints in the original edition of *La Trahison des clercs* that under,some circumstances Benda would allow the intellectuals to enter the political arena without betraying. In general, however, the correct way for the *clerc* to act in the modern world is to protest vocally, then submit and drink the hemlock when the State so orders. Any other action is treasonous. H. Stuart Hughes' criticism seems justified: "Had they followed to the letter the advice Benda offered, few European intellectuals would have survived the two decades subsequent to the publication of his book."[68]

Doubtless to Benda's delight, *La Trahison des clercs* immediately stirred up passionate controversy, and Benda produced a great deal of polemical journalism in the decade after 1927. He collected some of his best articles and published them in a volume entitled *Précision (1930-1937)*. Here we find a considerable evolution in Benda's thought on the subject of political involvement of the *clercs*, a movement not exactly toward compromise, but toward some recognition that the realities of modernity had to be faced in new ways. He tried to maintain continuity with his earlier positions by including a prefatory note explaining that he had chosen articles which dealt primarily with critiques of *La Trahison des clercs*. These attacks had helped him to clarify his own positions, and he asserts that the articles selected were not mere sallies. The immediate subject was to serve as a pretext for more universal considerations.[69]

The promised emphasis on universal problems in *Précision* is very hard to detect. Benda ranges widely, from discussions of educational policy and nationalism to a strong attack on marriage as one of the greatest betrayals of the modern *clerc*, since the *clerc* should reduce his "temporal surface" to a minimum.[70] In some of the articles, however, the major themes of *La Trahison des clercs* are reexamined, first in a renewed attack on rightist *clercs* like Barrès, then in a more detailed treatment of the distinction between political speculation and immediate political action. Benda argues that there is a profound difference between the theoretical political analyses of the great *clercs* of the past and the conviction of many contemporary (1932) intellectuals that they are the "saviors" of society.[71] The true task of the intellectuals remains ". . . to think correctly and to find truth, without concern for what will happen to the planet as a result."[72]

Yet as the 1930s wore on, Benda participated in the general movement toward engagement which is such an important phenomenon in the intellectual history of that decade.[73] He began to sign leftist manifestoes, becoming for a time a "fellow traveler," what the French call a *compagnon de route* of the French Communist Party.[74] In *Précision* Benda tried to explain that he was not betraying by asserting that he would join such appeals only when they seemed to defend "eternal principles."[75] The *clerc* must preach justice and truth without regard for the practical consequences of his position. Even in a totalitarian age Benda demands a strict idealism. It is natural to compromise, but the intellectual must ". . . *elevate himself above that which is natural*."[76] He retained enough optimism to believe that continuous pressure on political leaders can have some effect, can constrain them to be partially just. "History is made from shreds (*lambeaux*) of justice which the intellectual has torn from the politician."[77]

Paul Nizan is surely correct when he describes the Benda of the mid-thirties as a *clerc de gauche*.[78] Benda publicly stated that the *mystique de gauche* is acceptable for the *clerc*, as long as he does not descend into *la politique*.[79] The leftist mystique is noble whereas that of the Right is ugly because it honors force. Yet in the articles published in the early 1930s Benda still emphasizes repeatedly that he will strictly limit his collaboration with the communists. In an article dating from 1934 entitled "For Whom Do You Write?" Benda professes a real inability to grasp the arguments of revolutionary writers—Paul Nizan is the example he cites—who claim that an intellectual who is reserved and withdrawn from society is really aiding capitalism. Benda cannot see how writers like Paul Valéry and Jean Giraudoux ". . . serve the *Comité des Forges* or the powerful banking interests. Even less that they serve them consciously."[80]

The communist intellectuals attack the man "who meditates between his four walls" for not acting, even when his literary production "labors in the sense which is dear to them."[81] The communists should recognize that there is an element in a writer which remains outside the social regime, that in France there exists a long tradition of literary independence, that French writers will not make good militants, whether communist or fascist. Benda follows this logic to the extreme of stating that he had written his polemical works ". . . with the perfect conviction that they would not change my contemporaries, . . . and [in any case] I care very little about this changing."[82] In two hundred years some bibliophile—and he hopes that the species will still exist— might open his work and remark with surprise that in this universally pragmatic age here was one man who did not cooperate. Benda decides that he had been writing for such a judge.[83]

Benda recognizes the power of Paul Nizan's arguments for a communist humanism. Nizan only made him see more clearly how different his conception of humanism is. It is, he proclaims, based on classical culture, and he holds strongly to the dichotomy between spiritual and material life. The reconciliation of intellectual and manual labor holds little attraction for him, since man is great only when he obeys his "divine part." He has no sympathy for those who "drink life through all their pores."[84] Benda rejects contemporary left-leaning writers like Jean Guéhenno and Jean-Richard Bloch who call for humane rather than intellectual values. He prefers emaciated figures who lived the pure life of the spirit, and cites as examples Dante, Erasmus, Fénelon, and Pope Leo XIII. For Benda the Marxist-inspired religion of "total" man is merely a revitalized romanticism, venerating passion and action. There is no such creature as a "total" philosopher; one practices philosophy only "with the spirit."[85] Spiritual and economic activities are totally distinct, and therefore his humanism demands the autonomy of the spiritual life, freedom for the spirit to escape society, even to act against society, to challenge any "established order."[86] Benda realizes that he has the communists, the Hitlerians, and the *Action Française* against him, and the reader may perceive a certain nobility in his isolation, in his determination to retain his vision of classical humanism. It seems clear that if he had not been fettered by his idealism,[87] if it were not for his adhesion to the classical (and in his view eternal) values of truth, justice, and reason, he would have gone the whole route and joined the Communist Party.

As the decade of the thirties progressed, "his scruples did fall away,"[88] though never completely. He felt obliged to confront a new question; how should the *clerc* respond in an extreme situation, when two equally brutal factions exist and are clashing with such violence that one must inevitably crush the other and dominate Europe if not the world? Benda phrased this question in a note first published in January 1937 in the *Nouvelle Revue française*. His response shows a substantial change since 1934 in his attitude toward communism and toward political involvement, though one can find a slender thread of continuity even with *La Trahison des clercs* (because, as we have seen, Benda admitted in the earlier work that the existence of absolute injustice validates involvement).

By 1937 Benda has actually become *critical* of the intellectual who remains in monastic isolation, pursuing his disinterested labor of science, poetry, or philosophy! In a very striking statement, which would not have sounded out of place had it appeared in Jean-Paul Sartre's *Les Temps modernes* after the Second World War,[89] Benda wrote:

I say that the *clerc* must now take sides. He must choose the side which, if it threatens liberty, at least threatens it in order to give bread to all men, and not for the benefit of wealthy exploiters. He will choose the side of which, if it must kill, will kill the oppressors and not the oppressed.

The *clerc* must take sides with this group of violent men, since he has only the choice between their triumph or that of the others. He will give them [the com-

munists] his signature. Perhaps his life. But he will retain
the right to judge them. He will keep his critical spirit.[90]

By 1938, Benda went as far as to claim that through their
actions and the policies they advocated the communists were
the only truly patriotic party in France.[91] By keeping his
critical spirit intact and not joining the French Communist
Party, Benda probably spared himself a good deal of moral
anguish when the Nazi-Soviet Pact was signed at the end of
August 1939. Benda quickly denounced the pact as a *trahison*
in an article dated September 1, 1939.[92]

Despite suffering, exile, vicious anti-Semitic attacks by
the fascist intellectual Robert Brasillach ("circumcized
diplodocus" was one of Brasillach's more inventive and relatively mild insults),[93] and extreme old age Julien Benda managed to survive the Second World War and retain his critical
spirit. In June 1940 he fled Paris and barely escaped to Carcas-
sonne in the Vichy zone. The Germans seized his Paris apartment in 1941, and all his notes and his library were taken and
have never been recovered.[94] Benda held an entry visa for the
United States, where he had made a series of successful lecture tours in the years 1936-1938, but the Vichy government
refused to allow him to leave. In May 1944, his friends
warned him just in time and he escaped arrest by the Gestapo.
He managed to get to Toulouse, where he stayed until the
summer of 1945. During the Occupation his pen was of
course silenced, except for a few pieces which appeared in
clandestine resistance journals and a book published in New
York in 1942. As soon as he was free to publish again, a flow
of works that would have been impressive from a man half
his age began to appear. (Chambat lists fourteen full-length
books and the articles number in the hundreds.)

Neither the violent and terrible events of the two previous
decades, nor his shifts of position in the 1930s, nor his willingness to offer "tactical support"[95] to the communists from
1943 to 1950, could alter Benda's conviction that the initial
thesis of *La Trahison des clercs* had lost none of its truth. He

never saw, or at least never admitted, any contradiction between his passionate political commitment, which Paul Nizan and Pierre Chambat both categorize as "engagement,"[96] his vast journalistic output which dealt usually with day-to-day social and political issues, not "the eternal," and the fact that he is widely recognized as the leading spokesman in twentieth-century France "for the case against committed literature or thought."[97] In *Les Cahiers d'un clerc* (1950), he stated: "I could rewrite my *Trahison des clercs* exactly as I wrote it twenty years ago."[98]

When a new edition of *La Trahison des clercs* was published in 1947, Benda added an important introduction in which he emphasized that the *clercs* were still betraying their true function to the profit of practical interests. The practical interests he cites are the love of order, the monolithic state, the Communist Party (*sic*)[99] or collaboration during the 1940-1944 period. No excuses were valid; any *clerc* was treasonous if his realism led him to accept fascism as a "fact" at the moment of Hitler's greatest triumphs.[100] Benda eagerly joined the controversy over the "right to error," and was bitterly critical of intellectuals like François Mauriac who, even though they had impeccable resistance credentials, advocated the commutation of sentence for convicted collaborationist writers like Robert Brasillach.[101] Benda believed that Brasillach's execution was completely justified. No alienation of individual liberty is to be tolerated; the clerical ideal remains "disinterested thought," and any intellectual who abandons that ideal must face the consequences.[102] Thought must be "rigid" and adhere only to itself.[103]

Thus two decades later Benda's theoretical opposition to most forms of engagement remains as firm as it was in 1927. He does at this time clarify his view on democracy. The *clerc* can adopt, even proselytize for, the democratic system and still remain loyal, because democracy has never existed: ". . . with its sovereign values of individual liberty, justice, and truth, *it is not practical*."[104] The duty of the *clerc* remains constant. "When injustice becomes master of the world, and the

entire universe kneels before it, the *clerc* must remain standing
and confront it with the human conscience."[105]

THE FUTURE OF JULIEN BENDA AND
LA TRAHISON DES CLERCS

Students of intellectual history are well aware of the pitfalls in
trying to predict the influence of a scholar, artist, or other intellectual figure on future generations. One can never be certain that a forgotten author is really dead and buried, neatly in
place with a paragraph in the literary histories. Because external conditions become propitious, or perhaps through the effort of a few scholarly defenders, an author can quite sud-
denly be found relevant, cited and reprinted, translated and
talked about.

The first significant effort to pull Benda from oblivion was
made two years after his death by the critic René Etiemble. In
his preface to the third edition of *La Trahison des clercs* Etiemble emphasized Benda's belief that the true *clerc* will never say
"my country right or wrong." Etiemble suggests that in 1958
more French artists and intellectuals are ready to struggle for
universal values than in 1927.[106] Etiemble mentions professors and journalists, priests, the Archbishop of Algiers, even a
general. The opposition press took substantial risks to tell the
truth about the Algerian War, and the Catholic daily *La Croix*
rather belatedly published some articles which conferred
upon it the "honor" of being seized in Algeria.[107] There may
be truth in the notion that in his native country Benda always
retained what is best termed an "underground influence."
The French intellectuals who became involved in the movement to end the war and grant Algeria independence were
guided more by an outraged sense of justice than a desire for
power and prestige.[108]

As far as contemporary America is concerned, the ideas
Benda championed may be traced to three distinct areas of
our intellectual life, though his role in their formulation and
advocacy is rarely recognized. First, there is the notion of pro-

fessionalism, which is held by a substantial majority of the American academic community, and is quite close to the "pure" position advocated by Benda in *La Trahison des clercs*. The sense of working within a discipline, of striving for the admittedly impossible goal of perfection within that discipline, the conviction that this unremitting labor is *the* important task for the scholar and intellectual, would not be foreign to Benda. Nor would the belief that outside involvement is painful, unnecessary, and to be avoided whenever possible, and that the university is a sacred place where the quest for pure, nonutilitarian knowledge should be pursued—though Benda himself was never part of the French university system.

Second, the vocal attacks during the 1960s by America's dissident academicians on the "Establishment Intellectuals"—holders of government contracts, cabinet advisors, consultants of all varieties, those who perform military research—remind one of Benda's denunciation of the new generation of realist *clercs*.[109]

Finally, the political behavior of America's "Alienated Intellectual Elite," primarily in opposition to the Vietnam war, shows in its rationale a resemblance to the more activist strain in Benda's thought which has been discussed in this chapter.[110] The evidence strongly suggests that Benda could not really resolve the contradiction between his commitment and his scholarly detachment. That dilemma was shared by many intellectuals during the period of engagement in the 1960s, and there is no reason to suspect that the tension is any less present now that the balance in America has swung sharply back toward detachment. It is perhaps significant that *The Treason of the Intellectuals* has been back in print since January 1969 in a paperback edition.[111]

In France during the 1960s there was a steady flow of publications about Benda and several of his works were reprinted.[112] A fourth edition of *La Trahison des clercs* was published in 1975, with an important new introduction by André Lwoff. Lwoff, interestingly enough not a *littérateur* but a scientist and the winner of the Nobel Prize in Medicine, believes that *La Trahison des clercs* has withstood "the dual trial of time and of history." Because of what Lwoff calls the "atemporal character" of Julien Benda's masterwork,[113] it is safe to predict that Benda will continue to irritate, challenge, and enlighten future generations of intellectuals, in France and wherever his work is available.

III

◊◊◊◊◊◊◊◊

The Marxist Rebuttal:
Paul Nizan
and the Professors

◊◊◊◊◊◊◊◊

The *game* is no longer permissible, even if it is that of
the intelligence.

André Gide[1]

BENDA CONTRA NIZAN

Robert Niess wrote of Julien Benda: "His passion is the
source of his vitality and of his effect: his hatreds have given
him his books."[2] Though Benda never wavered in his conviction that a descent from a purer state had taken place, is it possible that the anger and pessimism which he used to such effect in denouncing *la trahison des clercs* were simply aroused by
more flagrant examples of what was always done in the past?
The Marxist argument, that philosophers and all other intellectuals have never ceased to defend specific social groups,
usually their own, has been powerfully stated by Paul Nizan
in his polemic against *Les Chiens de garde*—the academicians
who so subtly support the *status quo*. *Les Chiens de garde* (first
published in 1932, reprinted in 1965, and translated into English in 1972 as *The Watchdogs*) has been briefly discussed in
Chapter I, in relation to the roots of engagement. If we examine the work more closely, we discover that in large measure
it is a direct rebuttal to *La Trahison des clercs*.[3]

As an introduction to *Les Chiens de garde* Nizan cites without commentary an extract from a published debate between

Julien Benda and Dominique Parodi (1870-1955), an influential academic philosopher and author of the standard text of the day, *La Philosophie contemporaine en France*, which had reached three editions by 1925. Parodi is making a rather Byzantine effort to distinguish between the idea of the absolute and the idea of the eternal, and Benda retorts, "The eternal is static." There follows an excerpt from the contemporary press listing the work of a recent criminal court session in Hanoi, then of course French colonial territory. Twelve were condemned to death, eleven to forced labor, and 131 others were given lesser, though severe sentences. Thus Nizan graphically makes an unusual connection, suggesting that there is a relationship between two species of watchdogs, "pure" metaphysicians and judges. Later in *Les Chiens de garde*, while criticizing Benda, Nizan refers to him as shrewder than his fellow watchdogs; he at least claims to be interested in real human beings, but then backs away by adding that ". . . it is in deserting them that he serves them best."[4]

Julian Benda stated bluntly that he was capable of a "true ideological fanaticism," and that for pure ideological reasons he would have killed Henri Bergson (1859-1941), the immensely popular and successful metaphysician who had played such a role in the "revolt against positivism" of the 1890s.[5] Benda must have been surprised when Nizan in *Les Chiens de garde* linked him to Bergson, whom he had been attacking so fiercely for thirty years, identifying the two as "fraternal enemies."[6] Nizan makes a number of other references to the treason of the intellectuals, always in a sense contrary to that intended by Benda. These will be discussed later in this chapter.

Despite this most inauspicious beginning, Benda and Nizan, both prone to polemic and almost delighting in making influential enemies, retained a grudging respect for each other. In 1935, they participated in a debate on the nature of Marxist humanism,[7] and Benda gave Nizan a rare compliment by calling him an "intelligent and fair-minded opponent."[8] In 1937, Nizan reviewed two of Benda's books with subtlety and sympathy.[9] In an odd sense the political and intellectual trajectories of the two men, after starting from almost opposite points, converge briefly around 1939. What would have happened had Nizan not been killed at the age of thirty-five during the Battle of Dunkirk is difficult to predict. By that time Benda was so alienated from all modern trends in literature and philosophy that a real rapprochement is doubtful. Benda survived Nizan by sixteen years, and in 1946 forgot any remaining grievances and joined a group of distinguished intellectuals (including Jean-Paul Sartre, whom he dismissed scornfully elsewhere) in signing a public statement defending Nizan's memory against the attacks of Communist Party propagandists.[10] This gesture is especially striking since at this time Benda was cooperating closely with the French Communist Party on many issues.

These later developments do not alter the fact that in 1932 Paul Nizan gave Julien Benda a prominent place among the watchdogs. One could even argue that without *La Trahison des clercs* as a base point, Nizan would never have written *Les Chiens de garde*. The latter book is a crucial document in the literature of engagement, and merits careful analysis. What are Nizan's arguments against the professorial guardians of the *status quo*? Do they have any validity for later generations of intellectuals? Is there any justification for making a claim for Nizan similar to the one that André Lwoff makes for Benda? Has *Les Chiens de garde* withstood "the dual trial of time and of history"?[11]

A MAN WHO LIVED FOR AND THROUGH ENGAGEMENT

If meaningful answers are to be provided to the questions asked above, some background information is essential, since Nizan's extraordinary yet brief career has only begun to be known in this country. Paul Nizan was a communist for most of his adult life, and was also an extremely well-educated and cultivated man, fluent in several languages including Russian, Greek, and English. He was a superbly insightful literary critic, who wrote sensitive reviews of such authors as Faulkner, Erskine Caldwell, and Eugene O'Neill, helping to introduce them to a French audience. He possessed an effortless mastery of the writer's craft. Susan Suleiman has observed that in even the most polemical of Nizan's works one finds a "striking mélange of lyricism, irony, dry humor (sécheresse), and passion,"[12] and Sartre spoke of "his relaxed, dry, and beautiful style" (son beau style sec et négligent).[13] Despite Nizan's obvious intellectual importance—a good case can be made that he was the most brilliant intellectual to remain in the French Communist Party for an extensive period of time—there was a long interlude after his death in 1940 when he was almost totally ignored in his native country. Only in 1960 did his reputation begin to rise, when his first work, Aden Arabie, was reprinted with a long preface by Jean-Paul Sartre. In the United States what one French author has aptly termed Nizan's "posthumous life" began in 1968, when a translation of Aden Arabie was published.[14] By that time, a major effort to revive Nizan's memory was under way. In 1965, Les Chiens de garde was reprinted, as was Les Matérialistes de l'Antiquité, a collection of translations. A year later Nizan became the sixty-first French author to be honored with a volume in the "Classiques du XXe siècle" series, and an important collection, Paul Nizan, Intellectuel Communiste, edited by J.-J. Brochier, was published in 1967.[15] This volume contains a valuable biographical introduction, and unpublished correspondence from two periods of Nizan's life—his "escape" to Aden in 1926-1927, and his few months as a soldier in 1939-1940. Also included is a selection of articles from the vast volume of his journalistic output. In 1968 Nizan's last published novel, La Conspiration, was reprinted. This powerful work analyzes unsparingly both the revolutionary aspirations and the impotent failures and betrayals of alienated upper-middle class youth during the late 1920s. Readers today will find some haunting similarities in La Con-

spiration to the student movements of the 1960s.[16] The novel was first brought to the attention of an American audience in a stimulating article by W. D. Redfern, "A Vigorous Corpse: Paul Nizan and *La Conspiration*."[17] The article also appeared in 1968; one is not sure whether the "vigorous corpse" is Nizan, the novel, or both.

Since 1968 the flow of publications by and about Nizan has continued unabated.[18] Three of his works are now available in English translation, and W. D. Redfern has published an excellent full-length biography.[19] It seems doubtful that Nizan will ever reach a mass audience in this country, or be as popular with students here as André Malraux, Albert Camus, or Jean-Paul Sartre himself, but his admirers are not limited to narrow academic circles. They include reviewers for journals like the *New York Times Book Review* and the *New York Review of Books*.[20]

In addition to critical commentary on his novels by literary specialists,[21] a number of other elements of Nizan's intensely productive career have been studied. The most fascinating controversy connected with his name did not exist until a few months before his death, though it continues to the present day. This, of course, is the effort on the part of the French Communist Party (henceforth *PCF*) to brand him as a traitor and a coward, to distort his reputation, and then to erase his memory almost completely. "The communists," Sartre wrote, "do not believe in Hell; they believe in nothingness (*néant*)."[22] This incident has been quite well documented by a number of authors,[23] though I believe it could be examined profitably in more detail, as an illustration of how intellectual history can be subsumed under party history; in fact, in a perfect totalitarian state, the two would be identical.

Most commentators have concentrated on the posthumous furor over Nizan's name and reputation, and have not said much about his actual break with the Party in September 1939, without which there never would have been any controversy. The impression one gets is that it was easy and natural for Nizan to leave, given the historical circumstances of the Nazi-Soviet Pact.[24] Yet there is evidence to the contrary, suggesting that the decision must have been extremely painful and difficult. In his journalism from the 1930s Nizan frequently speaks of Party membership as the only option open to the intellectual who wants to be true to himself and to his profession. Of course, many intellectuals, of whom Louis Aragon is the most famous, remained in the Party and did not resign in protest over the Nazi-Soviet Pact. Another striking piece of evidence comes from *La Conspiration* (first published in 1938). In this novel Nizan portrays a party militant, Carré, said to be modeled after Paul Vaillant-Couturier, whom Nizan greatly admired. A noninvolved intellectual named Régnier hides Carré from the police; he does so because the two men served in the same unit in the First World War. However, Carré's rapport with Régnier was ". . . not as close as with his comrades in the Party—party loyalties are more powerful than the loyalties of death and blood, . . ."[25] A little later in the novel, while explaining to Régnier why he believes the Party to be correct in insisting that its intellectuals accept discipline, Carré argues against the intellectuals' old love of negation. Carré finds grandeur only in affirmation, while admitting that he has disagreed with the Party on matters of policy. In some cases he believes he may have been right; yet, he asks, should he contradict his very nature in the name of liberty of criticism?

> Fidelity has always seemed to me to be of a more pressing importance than the triumph, even at the price of a rupture, of one of my momentary political inflections.[26]

Carré, the most favorably drawn character in Nizan's novel, is describing and condemning *precisely* what Nizan himself was to do only a year later. It is reasonable to assume that the decision Nizan made in September 1939 was not taken lightly; the question of why it was made at all will be discussed later, as it is best seen in the perspective of *Les Chiens de garde*.

FROM APPRENTICE WATCHDOG TO MILITANT

There is one other issue which needs some elaboration before turning to *Les Chiens de garde*, and that is the very question of how such a polemic could come to be written. How could this young intellectual, who by class background, educational preparation at the elite *Ecole Normale Supérieure* (henceforth *ENS*), with his fluent acquaintance with the classics, would seem destined for a distinguished academic career, have become such a totally engaged militant? Why did he not keep his distance from politics all during the 1930s, as did his friend Sartre, who did not even vote in the Popular Front elections and took out his Teachers' Union card only with reluctance? How could he have surrendered his intellectual independence to follow the party line in his journalism, if not slavishly, at least quite closely? "There were times when Nizan was, undeniably and willingly, a Marxist journeyman."[27]

All authors agree that the primary reason for his later engagement lies in his flight to Aden, the British colony on the Red Sea, so acutely memorialized in *Aden Arabie*, his first book. He saw capitalist society there in all its nakedness, he saw undisguised colonialist oppression, he understood Europe better, where the social evils were hidden beneath a veneer of cultural and personal freedom. It is quite striking that Nizan was in fairly close contact with Antonin Besse, the leading businessman in Aden, and when his appointment as tutor to Besse's son expired was offered a position in the firm. Nizan comments on Besse, both in his correspondence and in *Aden Arabie*, as a person whom he detests yet pities, a selfmade yet unfinished individual, not a tranquil man despite his success, a man who deceives himself into thinking that he has freedom of action. "*Aden-Arabie* as a whole is a story of a near miss, . . ."[28] and Nizan begins to outline the steps leading to his own engagement just after his portrayal of Besse.

In some of the most eloquent passages of *Aden Arabie*, Nizan describes his plan to return to Europe, to fight what he knows best and could hurt the most.[29] Yet it must be remembered that he was disturbed and alienated before he left "this navel of the earth which perhaps is Paris."[30] Otherwise Nizan presumably would not have accepted an offer that his fellow *normalien* Jean-Albert Bédé had already turned down, and abandoned the comfortable life of a privileged scholarship student at the *ENS*. Jean-Paul Sartre, who knew Nizan very well at the time, documents this early alienation.[31]

Aden Arabie was first published in 1931, after Nizan became a communist, and so it may not be a completely accurate source for understanding the emotions which drove him to flee in 1926. Redfern is convinced that Nizan wrote a draft of the work while in Aden,[32] and even though some Marxist ideology may have been added later, Nizan surely captures some of his own feelings when he speaks of a generalized sense among the young that they are about to graduate into prison. He comments on the typical adolescents of the 1920s, whose childhood has been spent during the war years. They have a sense of *huis clos*, of hopelessness; so they (and he) have tried to escape: "There were so many evasions: so many doors leading nowhere."[33] Some tried a return to God, some tried poetry or romanticism or worship of art or even suicide. And then, concludes Nizan, there was the voyage, the old idea of escaping to the Orient which has had such an appeal to French intellectuals—from Baudelaire, Rimbaud, Gauguin, and Gide in the nineteenth century, to St. John Perse, Claudel, and Malraux in the twentieth. This list is mine. Nizan includes two Englishmen, Robert Louis Stevenson and Rupert Brooke, in his examples, and could have added Lawrence of Arabia. Nizan left for Aden just three years after Clara and André Malraux embarked on "The Indochina Adventure."[34]

If Nizan did indeed, as he claims in *Aden Arabie*, make a decision to become a communist militant while still in the Near East, it is curious that his letters to his fiancée back in France, published in 1967, show no militancy. In fact in this fascinating correspondence Nizan at times sounds rather snobbish,

perhaps more typical of the *normaliens* of his (or any) generation. He talks of his "habit of reading Valéry and of decipher-
ing the *Ethics* [of Spinoza]."[35] His letters are sprinkled with
references to Claudel, Pascal, Ecclesiastes on the vanity of
voyages, Nietzsche, and manifest a certain pleasure in showing off his classical knowledge. He moves in a circle of young
British intellectuals who can recite Latin and Greek verses,
and does not yet seem to be protesting the fact that they all
have certain "passwords," *mots de passe*, which demarcate
their superior class status.[36] After four months have elapsed,
he does write that distance and solitude are having an effect on
his judgments, producing a "violence which was foreign to
me."[37] In one letter he speaks of his concern with ". . . the
bolshevist *mystique*. This direction is attractive. It is one of my
directions. . . ."[38] He admits in a later letter that while a student in Paris he had performed the same sort of sterile intellectual exercises he was to criticize so savagely in *Les Chiens de
garde*.[39]

A close reading of Nizan's correspondence from Aden
shows little political awareness and provides only the slen-
derest of clues that upon his return he will join the ranks of
the *PCF*. In other words, there is not even a sense of movement toward a position which would make him ready to take
the step into political involvement. He was distressed by
much of what he saw, but so were Sartre and Simone de
Beauvoir when they traveled around Europe in the mid-
thirties, especially in Greece in 1937. On the basis of this evidence, I would suggest that a very complex dual effect or
double step took place with Nizan, one that may show
similarities with the development of political consciousness in
other intellectuals.[40] His "escape" to a foreign environment is
to be sure the reason for his ultimate engagement, his adoption of the communist cause. Yet it was not until he returned
home that he saw clearly what the voyage to Aden had really
meant—which was, precisely, to reveal to him the truth
about his own old continent.

It should be recalled that Nizan's *ENS* training prepared

him to become a *lycée* professor, and that he did teach for one year before devoting himself full time to serving his party, primarily through his political journalism. His very attendance at the *ENS* automatically made him a member of France's intellectual elite. It is not surprising that beginning with *Aden Arabie* one of his central concerns was with education, and especially with how education relates to class structure in a capitalist society. In *Aden Arabie*, before the account of his voyage to the African continent, Nizan speaks briefly of his career at the *ENS*, of his conviction that the students there were elitist hypocrites. He also criticizes the teaching that was dispensed at the school; the professors had all made the great discovery that problems do not exist when terms are conveniently defined.[41]

Yet Nizan never lost his love for the classics, and found time to prepare a useful selection of his own translations of Democritus, Epicurus, and Lucretius, *Les Matérialistes de l'Antiquité*. Nor did he abandon his belief in the enriching value of culture for all humanity, and put his convictions into practice not only by a great deal of popular journalism but by teaching in a workers' university.[42] Culture can of course be defined in many ways, and Nizan attributes his own precise meaning to it. "Philosophy resembles medicine; there is thought which cures and thought which does not."[43] This idea is broadened to include all culture in an article first published in March 1935, "L'Ennemi public no. 1." The article deals with the social problem of illiteracy and then turns to an argument that culture is actually on the decline in France. "[True] culture has a critical function. Knowledge has a critical value."[44] Nizan goes on to stress his belief that culture aids one in attaining full consciousness of the social reality, and that such a consciousness has an ". . . explosive value. It can only lead to the will to transform [that social reality]. We are at an historical moment in which culture and knowledge have, more than ever, a directly revolutionary significance."[45]

The key question, which leads to the analysis of *Les Chiens de garde*, thus emerges. If genuine culture must lead to the attainment of a new consciousness, of a will to transform society, and thus to engagement, why does this not occur in most students, especially among the graduates of a school like the *ENS*? Nizan finds the answer in a complex, not always fully rationalized, deception on the part of the professors, the watchdogs.

THE WATCHDOGS

Nizan's primary focus in *Les Chiens de garde* is on teachers of philosophy, but it is clear that he intends his arguments to apply to all other disciplines. We shall examine these arguments in some detail. André Gide, though he recommended *Les Chiens de garde* to his sceptical friend Roger Martin du Gard, in defending his own evolution toward greater political involvement,[46] found the book badly put together and full of repetitions. "One has understood three times over what he wants to say, and still he continues to speak. But such as it is, the book is a sign of the times. The *game* is no longer permissible, even if it is that of the intelligence."[47] Gide's own flirtation with communism has been extensively documented, both by biographers and in his own *Journal*, his famous *Retour de l'URSS*, published immediately after his fateful trip to the Soviet Union in 1936, the *Retouches à mon Retour de l'URSS*, a reply to the vehement criticism stirred up by the first volume, and in the 1950 collection entitled *Littérature engagée*.[48] All agree that Gide had little understanding or sympathy for the doctrinal or theoretical aspects of Marxism, and Gide himself often admitted that he struggled valiantly with Marx but could never read him. It seems probable that Gide did not fully grasp what Nizan was attempting to do; the anger and the vitriolic denunciations appealed to him, but he did not see that Nizan was obliged to detail his documentation because he was trying to describe a very sophisticated system of maintaining social stability, backed up with elaborate intellectual constructs. Only Sartre and the existentialists, after World War II, began to develop and elaborate upon Nizan's analyses, and much of Nizan sounds as modern as Herbert Marcuse.

The first question Nizan deals with in *Les Chiens de garde* is, can one continue to study philosophy without any sense of the meaning and direction of his research? He wants to debate this question openly, since many young people are engaged in philosophical studies—often motivated merely by the vague notion that philosophy involves "good intentions" toward humanity, and that through the pursuit of philosophy peace will spread among men of good will. It is not quite so simple, Nizan argues, reminding his readers that a number of men have paid with their lives or their freedom for the practice of philosophy.

Nizan's first premise is that some philosophies are beneficial to mankind, and that others are fatal. There is no generally utilitarian Philosophy. Just studying formal philosophy will not benefit the human species, does not automatically put one in a more noble category of men. His teachers at the *ENS* wanted him to keep this illusion, "so agreeable to themselves." They were perpetuating the "myth of the clericature," Nizan claims, with Julien Benda obviously in mind.[49] They will continue to receive the Legion of Honor for obscure publications, though Nizan hopes not forever. If there is no single philosophy *en soi*, there must be instead a whole series of philosophies, just as there are Arabs, Frenchmen, etc. A philosophical system is, after all, an effort to unify and structure different elements; it is not and never was *univoque*, but is always *équivoque*. The only common element in the diverse philosophies which have appeared throughout the span of human history is an "entity of discourse," and one could add that they have a "formal unity of aim," in that they all claim to be able to formulate "dispositions and directions for human life."[50]

Thus Nizan has proven to his satisfaction that philosophy remains equivocal. One enterprise for critical thought would be to define the current equivocations surrounding the word "philosophy," since it can be assumed that there will be variations in each generation. If, despite the argument Nizan has presented, one still holds the view that philosophy is univocal, and if one finds the doctrines of Henri Bergson or some other popular and respected philosopher repugnant, one is forced to say that this is merely a "temporary deviation," an accidental sickness in *"la Philosophie éternelle."*[51] For Nizan the explanation is much more simple: Bergson, Parodi, Boutroux, and the other professionals belong tó a family of philosophers whom he regards as the enemy. How and why, he will explain in a later part of his book; definitely not for Bendaesque reasons—that is, not because he has a different vision of the eternal destination of philosophy. "I have no confidence in destiny."[52]

Nizan takes the antipositivist position, rather widely accepted today but quite unique in his time, that intelligence *per se* can be used for or against mankind. Intelligence is after all only a servant. As he puts it, on one side there are the idealist philosophers who emit truths about man, and on the other "the map of the incidence of tuberculosis in Paris which says how men die. . . ."[53] He gives other examples of the professionals' emphasis on elegance of argument, technical subtlety, a high (*hautaine*) manner of philosophizing, and urges students not to wander onto the "polished paths" and "frozen corridors" of a spiritualist philosophy.

As far as the relationship of these philosophers to contemporary history is concerned, they profess to live apart from other social groups, to be free from passing time and the chains of locality (*emplacement*). They are a "head without a body."[54] They abstain from reality, live in a state of "scandalous absence," are "lighter than angels" with their abstract definitions of liberty.[55] Nizan has already tried to show that all philosophies possess a temporal and human significance, despite the protestations of the academic philosophers, who either attack or totally ignore thinkers such as Marx who want to change, not interpret the world. "The decision simply to look passively at the world is as much an earthly decision made by philosophy as the decision to change the world."[56] Nizan later stresses that if individuals resign from active life, they are making *décisions de partisan*. "Abstention is a choice,"[57] and even the uneducated person is aware of this truth. The so-called purity of the philosopher is imaginary; every one of them, and Nizan means to include even Julien Benda, "participates in the impure actuality of his time."[58] The arguments I have just outlined were very frequently expressed by student activists and others in the late sixties and into the early seventies. Few realized that Nizan, if not the first to formulate them, was at least the first to phrase them in terms so strikingly appropriate to that time, so immediately accessible to a later generation of militants. The more direct source was, as would be expected, Jean-Paul Sartre, especially his *What is Literature?* When Staughton Lynd spoke to the first large anti-Vietnam war demonstration in Washington, D.C., on April 17, 1965, he said: "We are here today on behalf of Jean-Paul Sartre. . . ."[59]

Returning to the source of so many of Sartre's ideas on engagement, we find that after arguing that philosophy is equivocal and that philosophers cannot escape the actuality of their time, Nizan in *Les Chiens de garde* turns to a third major point. He now attempts to explain the philosophers' emphasis on timelessness and abstraction in Marxist terms. There is nothing mysterious or occult about it; it is simply an element of "bourgeois thought."[60] Men like Henri Bergson and Léon Brunschvicg (at the time a wealthy and eminent idealist philosopher with his own *hôtel particulier*)[61] live very comfortably, accept and love "the present order." They shun any philosophical conclusions potentially detrimental to that order. Always they strive to remain within the strict terms of their philosophical systems, and claim to be responsible only to their colleagues, "present and to come."[62] In a rather sardonic aside, which might be contrasted to Julien Benda's complaint that modern realist *clercs* would approve the judges of Socrates, Nizan asserts that the only reason current philosophers are angry over Socrates' condemnation is that his judges were not professional specialists in the field. Nizan rejects this narrow elitism and demands a real philosophical democracy.

One way Nizan illustrates his hypotheses concerning what really motivates the intellectual leaders of his day is to point up the tremendous contradictions between what these "pure spirits" promise, between their high ideals, and what they produce. He takes as an example their reactions to the First World War; they have not really considered the war, have not tried to measure this terrible event. During the actual years of conflict, they did what the generals commanded; if they were too old to be mobilized they "followed with docility the ignorant popular movements and exorted those who were mobilisable to die. . . ."[63] Each of their dead students was a "witness for their philosophy." Bergson saw the victory of France as his victory; the Marne seemed to Brunschvicg a "striking verification of his philosophy."[64] In other words, when they did get involved, they labored on behalf of the established order, the moderate to conservative bourgeois Third Republic. Nizan feels that it is time to get these men into a corner and force some straight answers from them. What are their thoughts on war, colonialism, factories, love, unemployment, suicide, abortion? They are not really deceiving anyone any more; if they refuse to take sides, it is apparent that the particular kind of partisan decision they have made is to support the *status quo*. They live well within society as now constituted, they have opted for "their spiritual comfort, and for the temporal guarantees of that comfort. . . ."[65]

Already in 1932, before liberal intellectuals became widely involved in antifascist leagues, and two years before the Popular Front movement began to gather real momentum, Nizan found that unusual pressures were mounting against the *clercs*. Concrete problems from the outside world were imposing more and more upon the consciousness of the *clercs*, seriously disturbing them. (Nizan uses Benda's term.) The equivocations of a man like Benda himself provide a striking illustration of the development Nizan is foreshadowing. Gide, of course, reacted by moving toward nearly full engagement, and even Roger Martin du Gard became more involved politically in the 1930s.[66] Most of the intellectuals, Nizan continues, will try to drive these real historical problems out of their minds by spending all their time learning a method, never attacking a particular situation, never approving or condemning, never engaging themselves. It is important to emphasize that at this point in his argument Nizan is criticizing intellectuals whose general political orientation would be categorized as "liberal," not fascists or even conservatives. This group that he has singled out will remain in general "docile *clercs*" of the bourgeoisie. Such individuals might become disgusted with the bombardment of "Tonkinese villages" (the French were already using aviation in Vietnam), and sometimes they will "ease with little cost their conscience by sending petitions which beg for clemency from those in power."[67] Nizan believes that these vague engagements and petitions work really to the advantage of those holding power. His statements are especially fascinating when considered in the context of the role of American intellectuals in the protest movement against the Vietnam War, from 1964 until the settlement in 1973. Nizan would clearly have had nothing but scorn for those who salved their guilt by an occasional peace march and a signature among thousands in an advertisement in the *New York Times*.

The question of what then *does* constitute viable political involvement for the intellectual is a key theme in *Les Chiens de garde* and in many of Nizan's other writings.[68] His essential point is that he believes it almost impossible for intellectuals to carry the revulsion they may feel upon learning of some incident—perhaps a colonialist atrocity—to any sort of conclusion. They are content with mere "outlines of indignation, of revolt." They cannot go as far as a "radical refusal," which might mean a refusal of their comfort, security, order, even their lives. "To renounce themselves. To wish for the annihilation of their own nature."[69] George Orwell was one of the few in the 1930s who understood the full implications of this argument.[70] Most intellectuals, Nizan continues, cannot admit the real aims and essence of their own class; so they throw up clouds of reasoning like a smoke screen, and end by searching for validating reasons for bourgeois domination, for stock dividends and all the rest. Of course Nizan himself had a solution, the classical Marxist one. The intellectual must finally opt for the party of the oppressed and for revolution. We remember that this solution worked for him only until 1939.

Nizan would be pleased if as a first step the academic philosophers could admit that "Any philosophy is an act. M. Parodi himself knows that every thought is an action."[71] (Parodi, we recall, was the philosopher whose debate with Benda is cited by Nizan as an epigraph to *Les Chiens de garde*.) The time has come, Nizan feels, to mount an offensive against these academics, a really revolutionary action of demolishing. It must be stated openly that college teachers, in fact the whole university system, which in France is a public institution, the professors being paid functionaries of the State, operate for exactly the same purposes as do generals, politicians, and the like. The professors are involved in a more subtle form of domination; they try to win over by persuasion. The University has taken over the role of the Church in the *Ancien Régime*—the University is the "spiritual lever of the state."[72] The eminent professors are the new bishops and cardinals; they are not innocent old men, but are identical to police at a demonstration, only with less naked power. The philosophers and other professors try to persuade young men and women to ignore social, political, and economic realities. One of their sources of power is their service as government inspectors who determine the careers of young teachers within the system. Perhaps because he assumed his readers would know, Nizan does not bother to mention a most telling example—Parodi himself was appointed Inspector-General of Public Instruction in 1919. The French intellectual leaders of 1932, Nizan adds, have an elaborate quasi-official doctrine, one of obedience, a lay positivism, a dedication to the *status quo*.[73] (Despite war, defeat, three changes of regime, decolonization, and the May upheavals of 1968, which began as a protest against perceived injustices within the university system, the situation described by Nizan has not changed that much. There are similarities between the French system and the somewhat less structured American arrangement, with the senior professors at the annual disciplinary conventions, surrounded by coteries of graduate students searching for employment. Since 1968 the French have tried to break out of their mold; it is unclear whether the Haby reform proposals will succeed. Whether the recent efforts to make the American system more democratic, to break the "old boy" networks through affirmative action legislation, requirements that openings be advertised, etc., have been effective is also an open question. One can assume that Nizan would argue that in a time of recession and retrenchment in the American educational "industry," the power of the senior professors, a group he would identify as an especially influential breed of watchdogs, has actually increased.)

Because of his Marxist convictions, Nizan was certain that the period of upheaval which began in 1929 with the onset of the Great Depression was not a temporary deviation. He assumed that the epoch of bourgeois domination was nearing its end. Still the intellectuals had not, for the most part, made a move away from their silence and their abstractions. Should they feel these pressures too strongly, Nizan predicted that reactionary philosophies would take up the slack in a last ditch stand—some form of fascist doctrine would be adopted by many intellectuals. Nizan was not far off the mark here, and the number of prominent European intellectuals who succumbed to "the fascist temptation" is larger than is sometimes recognized. George L. Mosse noted in 1968 that "the obvious attraction which fascism could exercise upon the creative intellectual is often overlooked."[74] In the French case one could cite among others Pierre Drieu la Rochelle or Nizan's fellow *normalien* Robert Brasillach as examples validating his prediction, and fascist engagement will be discussed in the next chapter. Nizan also thought that Social Catholic groups such as the personalists grouped around Emmanuel Mounier and *Esprit* would find themselves forced into the fascist camp, both by events and by the inherent contradictions of their doctrines.[75] On the other side, Nizan believed, communism would stand.

In his conclusion to *Les Chiens de garde*, Nizan makes his rebuttal to Julien Benda's *La Trahison des clercs* even more explicit, by asserting forcefully that to remain faithful to abstract clerical ideals is a *trahison*, a pretended fidelity which, by offering spiritual salvation to those who receive physical blows, hides a "supreme desertion." This infidelity to humanity is the "true *trahison des clercs*."[76] What Nizan calls for is another form of betrayal—that of one's own class. The cultivation of intelligence is a weapon, and in the universities young people are learning to use it, to turn against their parents, to hasten the death of the old world. They will be useful and not just apostles, they will become revolutionaries of the type described by Lenin, and the creation of values will come after the revolution. For the moment, the intellectual must cooperate completely with the working-class movement, in practical, day-to-day tasks. The philosopher should become a new variety of specialist, an expert in the indignation of the exploited, skilled in the denunciation of illusions and false perceptions—in reality a variety of propagandist (though Nizan does not go as far as to use the latter term).

> In a world brutally divided into masters and servants, we must at last frankly admit a hidden alliance with the masters, or proclaim our allegiance to the party of the servants. No place is left for the impartiality of the *clerc*. Nothing remains but the combats of partisans.[77]

One is either with the bourgeoisie or the proletariat. The time of ruse is over; one cannot hide under veils of Eternity, Reason, Justice. If philosophers today blush in admitting that they have betrayed mankind for the bourgeoisie, if we betray the bourgeoisie for mankind, "let us not blush in admitting that we are traitors."[78]

This is the concluding line of *Les Chiens de garde*, and the link to Julien Benda is obvious. It is also easy to see how Nizan laid himself open to the official *PCF* attack on him; the philosopher Henri Lefebvre, who had been a close colleague of Nizan's in the 1930s, did not have much difficulty in finding treachery in all his work.[79] The theme of betrayal *is* in fact present in much of Nizan's writing, not just in *Les Chiens de garde*. It is especially strong in *Antoine Bloyé*, the story of a man, said to be modeled after Nizan's father, who betrays the working class for the bourgeoisie, and in *La Conspiration*. The latter novel, the most mature of Nizan's works to have survived, delineates a complex series of betrayals on several levels, besides the obvious example of the character Pluvidage, who becomes a police informer and discloses the whereabouts of the communist leader Carré to the authorities.

VARIETIES OF TREASON

It is clear that Nizan *was* a traitor, but only in the sense of breaking with his Party over a crucial matter of policy. The Party has never produced the slightest shred of evidence to substantiate the extravagant claims its apologists made in the aftermath of World War II—that Nizan sold secrets to the Quai d'Orsay, etc. Like many others he simply could not accept the Nazi-Soviet Pact. To the end of his life he always claimed that he remained a communist. As is well known, he received a sort of posthumous justification in that the *PCF* did a complete about-face when Hitler invaded the Soviet Union in 1941. The shameful episode of neutrality toward, if not real collaboration with, Hitler was conveniently forgotten, resistance became the catchword, and the *PCF* could with substantial justification proclaim itself after the Liberation to be the "party of the executed" (*le parti des fusillés*).

Nizan's first biographer, Ariel Ginsbourg, predicted in 1966 that Nizan would eventually be fully rehabilitated by the *PCF*.[80] This has not yet occurred. While the Western European communist parties have become more independent of Moscow in recent years, developing the doctrine of "Eurocommunism," which has been severely criticized by the official party organs in the USSR, it is unclear whether this independence will be reflected in "local" intellectual matters. Given Roger Garaudy's exclusion from the *PCF* in 1970, one may question Ginsbourg's optimism with regard to Nizan. Garaudy, for thirty-six years the most loyal of party militants, author of nineteen orthodox books, the man favored by the leadership to do battle with renegades and bring recalcitrants into line, finally began to make his break after the Soviet reoccupation of Czechoslovakia in the summer of 1968.[81] In sum, Paul Nizan was a traitor to the *PCF* as Roger Garaudy is now a traitor, or for that matter Henri Lefebvre, who after he was himself expelled from the Party in 1958, admitted that he had helped to fabricate some of the charges against Nizan.

Suppose Nizan had survived the Battle of France. Would he have returned to the ranks of the *PCF* during the Resistance, as Sartre is inclined to believe?[82] This is, of course, an open question. There are very few, if any, examples of an intellectual's resubmitting himself to party discipline after a break as total as Nizan's had been made. And for that matter the Party would itself have been loathe to accept him, and surely would never have granted him an important position. It seems more likely that Nizan would have followed an independent leftist line, such as Sartre did after World War II, and that he, too, would have emerged as a significant intellectual leader and as a major force in French and European letters.

Some evidence against Sartre's hypothesis about his friend can be found in Nizan's own writings, even before he left the Party. In his preface to *Les Matérialistes de l'Antiquité* (published in 1936,[83] at the height of the Popular Front euphoria, before the Great Purges in Russia, and thus at the moment

when Nizan's party loyalty should have been strongest!),
Nizan observes that "there are certain epochs when all human
possessions, the values which define a civilization, crum-
ble."[84] He finds parallels between the age of Epicurus (341-
271 B.C.) and his own. During a period of debacle such as that
witnessed by Epicurus, one could only remain alone, whereas
in Plato's time it had still been possible, Nizan argues, to wish
for "the collective salvation of society." In the oppressive and
violent world Epicurus knew, "one could no longer hope for
anything save the salvation of the individual man."[85] Nizan
emphasizes Epicurus' doctrine of separation from society, the
social pessimism which led him to write: "The wise man will
not practice politics."[86] Nizan uses the word "secession" to
synthesize Epicurus' views. A wise man will secede from active life, from the savage struggles within the Athenian *polis*,
and from the official religions. Epicurus could not think in
terms of a revolution to produce the external conditions
necessary for psychological well-being; he merely puts society in parentheses, secedes from all conceivable societies.
Given the economic and technological level of Hellenistic
Greece, Epicurus could only envisage a personal, inwardly directed solution; no dream of a utopia was worth pursuing, no
"collective happiness." Epicurus did try to aid his disciples to
escape the fear of death and of time, and Nizan admired him
for constructing the bases of materialism, for inventing a universe without gods and supernatural laws. For the first time
theories of immortality are rejected, and man is "at last solitary and free among material objects."[87] Finally man can be
sufficient unto himself, and in this sense Nizan views Epicurus as a real radical. He concludes that today's materialist wisdom is not so very different from that taught by Epicurus,
"but that it would be much more ambitious."[88]

The last text Nizan selected for his anthology is an excerpt
from Epicurus on *ataraxia*, the state of undisturbed or un-
bothered soul, a kind of tranquility which is almost identical
in Epicurus with pleasure. *Ataraxia* is attained when the individual no longer fears death or the unknown, the eclipses, and
other portents which so terrified the Ancients. The knowl-

edge which comes through an awareness of multiple causation of phenomena leads to *ataraxia*. In a fascinating footnote, Nizan adds that what is imperative is to show that terrifying phenomena have a natural cause. The demonstration of the link between science and wisdom may be the highest lesson of Epicureanism. "If man wishes to be liberated, he will find his liberation *only* in knowledge (*la connaissance*) capable of uncovering for him a world without demons, without phantoms."[89] It is very likely that by September 1939 Nizan believed that the world of the *PCF* included demons and phantoms, and this belief was a major reason why he could no longer stay in the Party.

How deeply involved Nizan's moral sentiments were in his decision to resign from the *PCF* is another unresolved question. Sartre and others who knew him well feel that in reality he was profoundly and personally hurt,[90] that he was also furious because he was as unaware of the impending Nazi-Soviet Pact as was the average citizen. Nizan was not a man who could stomach compromises, as one can see as early as 1933 from his repudiation of a "united front" of disenchanted young intellectuals. He rejects all solidarity with other young nonconformist intellectuals such as the personalist Denis de Rougemont. According to Nizan the effort to lump together such disparate individuals constitutes both foggy reasoning and a political maneuver to stress the confusion of the youthful rebels. The communists, Nizan writes in January 1933, are not going to establish ". . . a united front with anybody who comes along, *we shall not conclude agreements, even temporary ones, with our most authentic enemies.*"[91] Even when it became the official Party line during the Popular Front, he was very hesitant and sceptical about cooperating with the Catholic Left. Since the Party leader, Maurice Thorez, had insisted on a dialogue with the Catholics, Nizan cannot reject any cooperation out of hand, but he does question whether an accord is possible, "even for limited ends." The doctrinal differences between the two groups are "irreducible," and there can be no "theoretical passage from one doctrine to the other."[92]

In a 1935 review of André Malraux's *Le Temps du mépris*,

Nizan termed Nazism "the farthest reaching attempt to crush down and humiliate humanity that history has ever known," and was willing to retreat into caves, if necessary, to struggle against this evil.[93] That an element of moral outrage was present in Nizan's response to the Nazi-Soviet Pact seems undeniable, and the sharpness and concision of the note of resignation he sent to Jacques Duclos (the Party's second-in-command) supports this conclusion. Its stinging tone appears especially in the original: *Je t'adresse ma démission du P. C. français. Ma situation de soldat mobilisé me dispense de rien ajouter de plus* ("I submit to you my resignation from the French Communist Party. My status as a mobilized soldier relieves me from adding anything more").[94]

However, Nizan himself claimed, both to his friends and in his letters from the Front to his wife, that emotions and a sense of morality were *not* involved.[95] To his wife Nizan wrote on October 22, 1939, criticizing some of those who were blinded by events and stayed in the Party. "At bottom, I believe I am right: only events will confirm or disprove me. But not arguments of a moral variety."[96] He argued that the French communists had blundered badly, had not shown *enough* political cynicism. The Russians were much more skilled in this area (i.e., it was to their particular national advantage to gain time in case of a later war with Hitler), and the French should have acted more independently and not followed Moscow so slavishly. Two days later he wrote stressing his belief that he would be proven correct. Sounding more and more like Epicurus (and closer to Julien Benda, who placed truth higher than justice or reason in his triad of values), Nizan seems to be adopting a personal—though an intellectual's—solution: ". . . I recognize only one virtue, neither courage, nor the will to martyrdom, nor abnegation, nor blindness, but only the will to understand. The only honor which is left to us is that of understanding."[97] He criticizes a certain comrade "G" who has a mystical faith in a miracle which will emanate from the USSR and save France. "When the mystification is over, we shall talk about it" (*nous nous expliquerons*).[98]

In the last months of his life, Nizan became sharply critical of the naive followers of Stalin: "They confound fidelity with silent adhesion to the hierarchy. A little too Roman and apostolic."[99]

When compared with the passage from *La Conspiration* cited earlier in this chapter, which also speaks of fidelity, this denunciation of his former associates shows how far Nizan has moved politically in a single year. Nizan's choice of words does, however, suggest a certain inner consistency. One element in his thought which remained absolutely constant was a very hostile attitude toward religion, especially Roman Catholicism, the religion of his childhood. Nizan's distaste for religion is perhaps most graphically expressed in *Aden Arabie*, when he describes the view, as the boat bringing him home from Africa steamed toward the French coast. He saw ". . . the two most revolting objects on the face of the earth: a church, a prison."[100] A further explanation for Nizan's leaving the *PCF* would thus hinge on a subtle variant of the "God that Failed" theory. If, as *Les Matérialistes de l'Antiquité* and many of his critical writings suggest, Nizan, in Bendaesque fashion, always refused that final surrender, never totally abandoned his critical judgment, never made communism into a replacement God, then it would be logical for him to submit his resignation when he came to realize that his comrades were treating it as if it were.

Thus Nizan's final position was one of waiting, abstention, perhaps even "secession" in the manner of Epicurus. All doctrines of the religious variety are rejected, and the conviction that events will prove him right remains. Politically he adopted a form of "national communism," which he never had the opportunity to describe in detail. At the time of his death Nizan was working on an analytical study of communism, which given what we know of his talents would have been a brilliant work of Marxist revisionism. When Nizan was killed, he had also nearly completed a novel, *La Soirée de Somosierra*. His manuscripts were buried by an English soldier, and after the war efforts were made to recover them. These proved fruitless.

One lesson which emerges from Nizan's case is that it provides further support for an argument professional historians frequently make—that it is dangerous to try to draw close parallels between historical periods. No matter how tempting it might be we cannot directly apply what we have learned from Nizan's case to our own time or any other, even to the 1960s when engagement seemed on the upswing and when Nizan began to be studied seriously in France and elsewhere. A special condition prevailed in the years of Nizan's early manhood, in that there was an active, militant, and as yet relatively untainted party with parliamentary representation, a party which seemed to respond to the intellectuals' need for engagement.[101] During these years the *PCF* appealed to intellectuals and asserted that they could make a contribution of value. This courtship may have been lukewarm, shifting, and uncertain, but it existed nonetheless.[102] We remember that the solution Nizan posed for the intellectual worked only until 1939; he was not to be given time to define precisely what his new stance would be, how he would conceive of the intellectual's performing his task—"The only honor which is left to us is that of understanding"—without becoming a *chien de garde*.

Nevertheless, *Les Chiens de garde* and the entire corpus of Nizan's work are major documents in intellectual history, for at least two reasons. First, as has been briefly discussed in this chapter, they have had a significant though hidden influence on the New Left in the 1960s. Second, and more crucial in this context, Nizan not only articulates the concept of engagement for the first time, but also presents with unusual clarity and persuasiveness, again very early, probably for the first time, the argument that the result of the intellectual's rational reflection on his environment must lead to engagement. Or, at least, the awareness that engagement is an ethical imperative, and that any other course of action must involve betrayal. Because the particular direction that Nizan found appropriate for more than a decade has lost its validity, probably permanently, the engagement of the intellectual, in the West at least, involves far more complications and uncertainties.[103] In some ways this may be a better situation, even if it tends to render the intellectual impotent, eternally unable to choose. Nizan's own case, with its inherent drama and tragedy, provides a superb illustration of how extraordinarily difficult it is to separate engagement from *embrigadement*. There is nothing in Nizan's writings which would deny the possibility of the tables' being turned and of communist party intellectuals themselves, under certain conditions, becoming watchdogs. We may conclude by paraphrasing Raymond Aron and asking, "Once again, where are the Watchdogs?"

IV

◊◊◊◊◊◊◊◊

Fascist Engagement

◊◊◊◊◊◊◊◊

Je sais trop bien que la politique, c'est du sang.
                    Pierre Drieu la Rochelle[1]

Vous, le clerc qui avez trahi, . . .
                    Maître Reboul, the Prosecutor
                    at Robert Brasillach's trial[2]

PROBLEMS FOR THE SCHOLAR—ONE IS ALWAYS SOMEBODY ELSE'S FASCIST[3]

Paul Nizan predicted in 1932 that as increasing external pressures forced intellectuals out of their ivory towers, a significant number would take refuge in fascism. It is now a recognized, if still uncomfortable, fact that Nizan was correct, that the number of prominent European intellectuals who succumbed to "The Appeal of Fascism," who showed what John Hoberman has called "Sympathy for the Devil,"[4] was larger than has often been admitted. Already in 1943 George Orwell remarked that "the relationship between fascism and the literary intelligentsia badly needs investigation."[5] These investigations did indeed begin in the mid-fifties, and the volume of publication, dealing both with individuals and groups of intellectuals, has grown steadily.[6]

No study of intellectual engagement during the years 1920-1945 would be complete without a discussion of fascist political involvement. It might be possible to dismiss fascist engagement as merely another variant of *embrigadement*, more noxious for most than even the most unregenerate Stalinism. This, however, would evade the problem we have tried to face with regard to communist political involvement, namely the impossibility of finding objective criteria to distinguish between engagement and *embrigadement*.

If we are determined to proceed to study fascist engagement, we find ourselves almost immediately confronted with a veritable thicket of difficulties. By its very nature as a doctrine and as a political movement holding power in several European countries, fascism calls forth passionate reactions and still does so more than thirty years after the end of the Second World War.[7] Since 1945, politicians, journalists, and others have found the term "fascist" a convenient insult, and there has been a tendency, not only in France but also in the United States and elsewhere,[8] to label one's political enemies loosely as "fascist." Even rightist parties in France have found this a convenient political technique, and have denounced the Left as fascist, "turning against its inventors this redoubtable weapon. In brief one is always, or one has been, somebody's fascist" (*le fasciste de quelqu'un*).[9] This problem can be circumvented, if not totally avoided,[10] by following the method established by Plumyène and Lasierra in their excellent survey, *Les Fascismes français, 1923-1963*. Plumyène and Lasierra take the position that those individuals are fascist who openly "*so identify themselves.*"[11] They make a good case for this position, pointing out that Colonel de la Rocque, leader of the Croix-du-Feu movement in the 1930s, who was feared by the Popular Front as the symbol of French fascism, never publicly called himself a fascist. De la Rocque ended his checkered career by being deported during the Occupation for acts of resistance.[12] Thus we shall avoid using the term fascism interchangeably with monarchism, Bonapartism, nationalism, the extreme Right in general, and even with collaborationism.

Except for carefully specified cases, which will be cited for the purposes of comparison and illustration, the intellectuals discussed in this chapter will be self-proclaimed fascists whose period of activity as fascists was somewhere between 1920 and 1945. With regard to chronology, I shall follow Ernst Nolte and establish 1945 as a firm cut-off date. While scholars have and will debate endlessly about where the residues of fascism may be found in the world, the period when fascism could be seen as "characteristic of an era" ended with the fall of the Third Reich in May 1945.[13] Certainly as far as intellectuals are concerned, there are no surviving intellectual figures of the first or even the second rank who still identify themselves as fascists.[14] The last unrepentant fascist intellectual, of any recognized literary ability, was Lucien Rebatet, who died in 1972.[15]

With the problems of terminology and chronology resolved, or at least suspended to facilitate further analysis, we can turn to a far more difficult question, which has perhaps never been more eloquently stated than by George Steiner in his preface to a source collection on the French Right. Those who would study the appeal of fascism to intellectuals are faced with the "intractable puzzle of the co-existence in the same mind of profound inhumanity and obvious philosophical and literary importance."[16]

Of those French, indeed European, intellectuals who openly identified themselves as fascists, Robert Brasillach is one of the most fascinating and the most controversial. This is not only because of Brasillach's undeniable intellectual abilities, but because unlike Ezra Pound, who paid for the "fascistic zeal" of his more than three hundred radio broadcasts from Mussolini's Italy by incarceration in St. Elizabeth's Hospital for the Criminally Insane,[17] and unlike the great Norwegian writer Knut Hamsen (1859-1952), who—while perhaps never a true fascist but certainly a collaborator—was merely given an intensive psychiatric examination, a satiric account of which he was allowed to publish in 1949,[18] Robert Brasillach was tried "for intelligence with the enemy," sentenced to death, *and* executed. He was the only European fascist intellectual of stature to receive the death penalty.

The primary focus of this chapter will be a study of the Brasillach case. The reasons for its unending fascination have been brilliantly pointed out in an article by H. L. Wesseling, "Robert Brasillach and the Seductiveness of Fascism." After noting that the climate of opinion must be taken into consideration as an extenuating circumstance, that there were special pressures which drove all intellectuals toward political engagement in the 1930-1945 period, Wesseling suggests that there were two broad categories of intellectuals who were attracted specifically to fascism. The first route toward fascism is intellectually more comprehensible today, namely that followed by those intellectuals who "saw in the persistence of the economic crisis (of the 1930s) signs of irreversible crisis of capitalism and of the outdatedness of parliamentary democracy. Some found their new gods in communism, others in fascism: 'Gods that failed,' often."[19] The members of this group who turned rightward abandoned fascism or fascist tendencies rather quickly. Among them would be included T. S. Eliot, Wyndam Lewis, Paul Claudel, and many others.

Then there was the smaller group of those who were totally committed, "the more existential seekers and doubters." They saw behind the economic and political crisis of the 1930s an emergent struggle for a new type of person, *homo fascista*. Brasillach was an extreme example of this second type: "But the stubborn persistence in the evil, this was much rarer and seen intellectually, much more incomprehensible. Therefore there is a *'Brasillach riddle.'* From whence did this unwillingness to open up the new information, the inability to examine ideas, to reevaluate convictions in the light of new knowledge come?"[20]

While Brasillach has been the subject of several full-length biographies already, the best of which, by an American, William R. Tucker, is an intelligent, well-documented and deliberately dispassionate study, no serious writer has as yet directly faced the "Brasillach riddle." Tucker was present in France with the Allied Forces when Brasillach was executed, and became interested in the case and "the reasons behind Brasillach's behavior." This prompted him "to explore the *riddle of Brasillach's treason* further."[21] This similarity in terminology is striking, since both Wesseling and Tucker published their studies in 1975, were separated by an ocean and a language barrier, and were not aware of each other's work.

Tucker does indeed *describe* Brasillach's treason very carefully, and documents it thoroughly, with extensive and damaging citations from Brasillach's writings. But while he provides in the course of his analysis a number of interesting insights and suggestions,[22] he does not truly "explore the riddle of Brasillach's treason," does not answer the "why" of Brasillach's commitment to fascism.

Many scholars would agree that Tucker's approach is the correct one, that he is justified in not attempting to answer the question of "Why fascist engagement?" The practically instinctive reaction of the professional historian, if pressed further on the matter, would be to turn it over to the theologian or the psychoanalytic theorist. The historian could cite good reasons for taking this step, based on the widely recognized necessity for a degree of impartiality and objectivity. The historian's response would surely resemble that of the sociologist when asked about the nature of evil. As Kurt H. Wolff states in a superb programmatic essay, "For a Sociology of Evil," most social scientists would feel virtuous about not trying to answer such questions: " 'Of course,' they might put it, 'the exploration of the nature or essence or meaning of evil *obviously* is not our concern; it *is* a concern for the philosopher and the theologian! All we do and legitimately *can* do is ascertain (as well as possible) what man, what certain men *consider* evil. We study beliefs about evil, conceptions of it, attitudes toward it, the moral code of a given society or other group, . . .' "[23] Yet for Wolff such nominalism is inadequate; it commits us as scholars to a "science which claims *not* to know what evil is, *not* to be responsible for knowing it or seeking to know it, and which, they are convinced, would indeed lose its character of science if it founded its investigations of evil on its own conceptions of it."[24]

Can a path be found between polemics and pragmatism where the rigorous and patient application of the scholarly tools available to us will cast some light on George Steiner's "intractable puzzle"? Steiner, himself a distinguished member of the "intellectual migration" from Hitler's Europe which has so enriched our cultural life, believes that "because the political and philosophical programme of the Right has come so near to destroying our civilization and is alive still, it must be studied."[25] Can we strive, not to suppress our values in a vain quest for pure objectivity, a goal which historians at least since Carl Becker and Charles Beard if not since Benedetto Croce have recognized to be a "noble dream,"[26] but to insure that our values interfere as little as possible with the quest for new truths, for new modes of understanding?[27] Kurt Wolff, another eminent intellectual migrant, eloquently states the paradox which must be transcended if we are to continue:

> . . . to be silent about that which we cannot grasp is the only adequate mode of being; the only adequate mode of being before that which we cannot grasp is *not* to be silent about it. Between these contradictory truths lies our dilemma, for we neither can be silent nor speak; we must speak, but we cannot speak.[28]

AN EXEMPLARY TRIAL

In this undertaking a convenient approach is to follow the method utilized heretofore in this study (and advocated by H. L. Wesseling for the analysis of fascist political involvement), and consider fascist engagement in the broader context of the many historical pressures driving European intellectuals toward engagement in the 1930s, the ensuing wave of engagement, and the debate over engagement as exemplified in the arguments of Mounier, Benda, Nizan, and others. The "riddle" of Brasillach's treason will thus at least not appear in isolation. Before addressing the question of his motivation, his trial and sentencing will be set in broader historical perspective. Finally, because it raises so many profound questions relating to all varieties of engagement, the matter of the justice of the sentence imposed upon Brasillach will be examined at the end of this chapter.

Brasillach's trial took place on January 19, 1945, and a verdict was reached after five hours. The death sentence was carried out by a firing squad on February 6, 1945, a date which was surely chosen carefully by the French authorities as an object lesson to any other unrepentant French fascists. It marked the eleventh anniversary of the famous Paris riots which for many, including Brasillach himself, had signaled the rise of a true fascist movement in France.[29]

We are fortunate to have a complete published transcript of Brasillach's trial, prepared by his lawyer Jacques Isorni, a man of considerable talent and strong right-wing persuasions, who later became an active supporter of *Algérie française*. The accuracy of the transcript can be assumed; it has never been challenged and Isorni would have been liable to a lawsuit from the judge and the prosecuting attorney if he had altered the testimony in the published text.

The trial itself was extremely dramatic, and has already been studied extensively.[30] It has also served as the basis for a novel, *Les Fins dernières*, by Pierre de Boisdeffre (1952), which reproduces the transcript almost exactly, merely changing a few names and biographical details, even down to the penultimate moment when Brasillach's verdict (de Courty in the novel) is announced, and a voice in the courtroom cries out, "It is a shame," and the hero replies, "No, it is an honor!"[31]

Brasillach did not grovel or put the blame on others, as many of the defendants at Nuremberg were to do. The resistance newspaper *Combat*, then edited by Albert Camus, found Brasillach to be the first of the accused to give "the impression of dignity."[32] Simone de Beauvoir, who was present at the trial, admitted that regardless of the life Brasillach had led, and regardless of the reasons for the sentence imposed upon him, "the dignity with which he acted in that extreme situation commanded our respect at the moment when we wished so strongly to despise him. We desired the death of the editor of *Je suis partout*, not that of the man [in the dock] who gave himself up totally to dying well."[33]

Brasillach's trial will be better understood if we emphasize that this was indeed an "extreme situation," in that Brasillach was the only French fascist (or collaborationist, or both) intellectual of wide reputation and recognized talent whose execution was actually carried out during what is usually called the *épuration*, the series of trials—and in some cases summary executions—which followed the liberation of France. A close examination of the records has been made by Peter Novick in his useful study, *The Resistance versus Vichy*, and Novick discovered that of the ninety-five collaborators executed in Paris, fifty had been "torturers in the employ of the Germans or the *milice*, thirty had been informers." Some of the rest were journalists, but except for Brasillach, they were polemicists of negligible intellectual achievement.[34]

Given these facts, it is not surprising that Brasillach's defenders, and Brasillach himself while in prison, made much of the parallel with André Chénier, the French poet who was guillotined by the Jacobins in 1794, an early example of an intellectual's paying the supreme price for antirepublican engagement.[35] We shall return to this extremely interesting parallel later.

Brasillach was just thirty-five years old when he went on trial (one of the many ironies of this case is that Brasillach's father had been the same age when he died in the service of his country).[36] However, he had already accumulated an impressive bibliography, publishing more in his short career than many productive writers in a full lifetime. His biographer Pol Vandromme lists two volumes of poems, seven volumes of essays plus two unpublished, seven published novels, seven volumes of *Chroniques*, including the well-known *Histoire du cinéma*. The latter work, which he co-authored with his brother-in-law Maurice Bardèche, has been updated and reprinted several times since his death, issued in paperback, and translated into English. By 1970 an edition of his complete works had been brought out in twenty-eight volumes and 4,500 sets had been sold. The sales of his works in paperback by 1970 totaled an extraordinary 325,000![37] As a journalist Brasillach wrote for *l'Action française*, where at the very early age of twenty-two he was put in charge of the literary column,[38] *Candide, Révolution nationale, La Chronique de Paris*, and especially *Je suis partout*, which after his editorship began in 1936 became openly fascist, and when France fell became "the principal collaborationist political and literary weekly."[39]

Given the intellectual stature of the accused, M. Reboul, the *Commissaire du Gouvernement*, prepared an extraordinary address for the prosecution, sprinkled with literary allusions—to Pascal, Galileo, and Péguy among others—and thus quite foreign to those acquainted with Anglo-Saxon judicial systems and procedures. Reboul warned the judge and the jury that "Brasillach has presented himself to you [in his defense speech] gilded with all the seductions of the writer, and I shall say now that I have heard him, for I did not know him previously, gilded with all the seductions of persuasive eloquence."[40]

Reboul openly admits the defendant's literary talent; as a former student of the elite *Ecole Normale Supérieure*, Brasillach could already claim an "incontestable intellectual primacy." His skill as a critic is especially praised, and the wide influence of his judgments on modern literature is noted. M. Reboul then asks a profound and moving question, which is in truth a jurist's formulation of the "Brasillach riddle":

> Why did this man, rich with so many gifts, blessed with so much success, who could have, if he had remained in the line of his earliest aspirations, become one of the most eminent writers of our country, abuse those talents, that success, that authority, and try to lead our youth, first toward a sterile politique, then toward the enemy?[41]

As a prosecutor, M. Reboul is not interested in answering his own rhetorical question; his aim rather is to prove that Brasillach was not simply an idle poet or speculative theorist, but a dangerous polemicist and propagandist, someone who knowingly used his high talents, his ability for textual analysis, for evil purposes. There can be, Reboul claims, no extenuating circumstances, and in any case, "I suppose Brasillach is too prideful a person to claim them."[42]

The whole thrust of Reboul's speech, buttressed by citations from Brasillach's virulently anti-Semitic, antirepublican and even pro-Nazi journalism,[43] is to prove that a "trial of opinion" is not taking place, but the trial of a traitor, guilty of "intelligence with the enemy." The French Republic, Reboul asserts, now speaking directly to the defendant, "will not try you for your tragic errors, for your savage intolerance, for your subversive opinions, but it will, according to Article 75 of the Penal Code, and with the necessary proofs assembled, present to you, *le clerc qui avez trahi, le procès de votre trahison*" (the clerk who has betrayed, the trial of your treachery).[44] The reference to Julien Benda is obvious, and Benda as we have seen was not one to forgive his enemies. Benda could not have been in the audience as he did not return to Paris from where he had been in hiding in Toulouse until the summer of 1945, but he would have been pleased at the reference and found it completely apropos.

THE APPEAL

According to his defense lawyer, Brasillach appealed for executive clemency only to please his mother. His request was denied by General de Gaulle, under circumstances that remain somewhat mysterious, despite the fact that Brasillach was the only son of an officer who had been killed in combat in 1914, and despite a petition on his behalf signed by a number of leading literary figures, some of whom had been active in the Resistance.[45]

One of the intellectuals who supported clemency for Brasillach strongly was François Mauriac, who actually went as far as to seek a private interview with de Gaulle to plead on Brasillach's behalf. De Gaulle apparently told Mauriac that he could rest assured, Brasillach would not be executed. Something then intervened to make de Gaulle change his mind. Accounts are conflicting; Isorni thinks that the dossier may have been tampered with or that de Gaulle may have seen a picture of Jacques Doriot or someone else in a Nazi uniform and confused him with Brasillach.[46] Jean-Raymond Tournoux in his undocumented popular history, *Pétain et de Gaulle*, claims that Mme de Gaulle told him that her husband found this case the most difficult, lost sleep over it, and told her after he had made up his mind: "Brasillach gambled. He lost. He will pay. With his degree of intelligence he could not have been ignorant of what he was doing. Intellectual treason. Sinning against the spirit" (*La trahison intellectuelle. Le Péché contre l'esprit*).[47]

Perhaps de Gaulle did indeed say something like this, but he died without making any formal clarification. Officially, in discussing the trials of collaborators and Vichyites in the third volume of his *Mémoires de guerre*, de Gaulle does not mention Brasillach by name. He does specify that 2,071 death sentences were pronounced by the courts, in addition to those sentenced *in absentia*. The General states that he personally reviewed every dossier, and after receiving legal advice, made his decision in each case. "In conscience I can attest that, save for about a hundred cases, all of those condemned deserved to be executed. Nonetheless, I granted reprieves to 1,303 of them. . . ."[48] De Gaulle commuted the sentences of all the women and most minors, and most of those who acted upon formal orders and risked their lives. "I had to reject 768 pleas. These were the cases in which the spontaneous and personal action of the condemned had caused the death of other French citizens, or had directly served the enemy."[49] Thus, in the General's mind, Robert Brasillach must have belonged to the latter group. Of this much we can be certain.

THE MOTIVES

Hence the jurist can make the accusation of *trahison*, and the political leader with the power to act in the situation can decide that the accusation is justified, that *trahison* did indeed take place. It is neither their wish nor their function to attempt to answer the question "Why fascist engagement?" though the background information they can provide is valuable in setting the Brasillach case in its proper historical context. We should now be able to review some of the explanations that have been suggested by others, and to propose our own.

Romanticism

Several writers believe that the real reason for the political involvement of French fascist intellectuals lies in a loosely defined romanticism. The French fascists were simply incurable romantics, with a cult of passion and emotion, a sense of France's decadence, a need to worship heroes, to find some organic unity in a confused and divided modern world. Did not Robert Brasillach himself at least twice term fascism his "sickness of the century" (*mal du siècle*), borrowing a famous phrase from the romantic author Alfred de Musset?[50]

As one might expect, since our normal understanding of "romantic" implies emotion, lack of reasoned analysis, perhaps even childlike qualities, and thus less adult responsibility, apologists and admirers of Brasillach and like-minded intellectuals have wholeheartedly adopted the "romantic explanation."[51] For example, Paul Sérant has written a well-known study, *Le Romantisme fasciste* (1959), which deals with six writers, three of whom openly admitted being fascists, while the others had strong and widely recognized fascist inclinations. Romanticism is the common theme Sérant finds in these six very different, often contradictory intellectuals—Robert Brasillach, Pierre Drieu la Rochelle, Lucien Rebatet, Alphonse de Châteaubriant, Abel Bonnard, and Louis-Ferdinand Céline.[52]

Another work which equates fascism and romanticism is Pol Vandromme's completely adulatory biography of Robert Brasillach. The reader may tend to suspect Vandromme's judgments from the outset, since he makes the questionable claim of having "driven out *la politique* from this book."[53] Among Vandromme's highly political statements one might pick his characterization of the leaders of the Third Republic as *vermin*,[54] or his praise of Francisco Franco as a Spanish general "who engaged his country to sweep away a Popular

Front even more virulent than the one which had established itself in France."[55] Nonetheless, the book is useful for the detail it provides, since Vandromme had access to unpublished correspondence, and it does contain sharp insights into such matters as Brasillach's eventual break with his mentor Charles Maurras.

In his treatment of Brasillach's presumed romanticism, Vandromme pulls out all the stops; it is the central theme of his work. Three examples will suffice. First, Vandromme claims that the young Brasillach had tended to be Germanophobe, as had Charles Maurras, but when he visited Hitler's Germany he was "seized at first by the delicious and gentle romanticism of Germany."[56] Vandromme later asserts that even Brasillach's enemies will admit that there was in his political choice ". . . no vulgar motive—but the unrealism of the poet, the pressures of impetuous youth, a romanticism of force, of scouting, of friendship."[57] Finally, in his conclusions Vandromme argues that fascism was in effect "a cry which carried through the night and which promised to those who listened sanctuaries, incense, beautiful ornaments, saints of youth and priests which would exorcise from young men the demons of fear." Judges, intellectuals, and other social types will never understand the motivation of someone like Brasillach, who was "disinterested and pure." For him fascism was not really a doctrine, ". . . but a great movement of fever."[58]

A Clarification—the Case of
Drieu la Rochelle

Before analyzing the claim that Brasillach can be best understood as a perhaps somewhat wayward romantic, it will be useful to discuss briefly Pierre Drieu la Rochelle (1893-1945), another self-proclaimed fascist, and another in Paul Sérant's list of fascist romantics. Drieu la Rochelle was an important literary figure of the interwar period, a talented poet, novelist, and essayist. After a rather diverse early career, including service in the First World War, for which he was decorated, youthful literary success for a volume of war poems, and an interest in surrealism in the 1920s, Drieu was converted to fascism in 1934. In 1936 he joined Jacques Doriot's *Parti Populaire Français*, often said to be France's only authentic mass-based fascist party.[59] During the occupation Drieu collaborated extensively with the Nazis, becoming editor of France's most prestigious literary periodical, *La Nouvelle Revue française*. It is arguable that he, too, would have faced a firing squad, had not his third suicide attempt succeeded in March 1945. (He was in hiding at the time and had just learned that a warrant had been issued for his arrest.)[60]

Drieu la Rochelle's case is obviously dramatic and fascinating in its own right, but it has been well studied elsewhere.[61] It will be examined here strictly for the light it casts on Robert Brasillach, and particularly on Brasillach's presumed romanticism. A highly persuasive study of "fascist romanticism" has been published, dealing strictly with Drieu la Rochelle. The author, Robert Soucy, made a close examination of Drieu's work and concluded that there were indeed some romantic elements present, such as his praise of irrationalism, his admiration for the Middle Ages, and the worship of passion in novels like *L'Homme à cheval* (1943, a fantasy about a South American dictator). Soucy also noted that Drieu glorified the return to nature, viewing fascist man as a kind of "modern noble savage."[62] Soucy could have also pointed to Drieu's fascination with suicide, a common theme in many of his later works and the subject of one of his most powerful novels, *Le Feu follet*, published in 1931 and based on the suicide of Jacques Rigaut which occurred in 1929.[63] Suicide is a quintessentially romantic theme, going back at least to the wave of suicides that followed the publication of Goethe's *Werther*.

Robert Soucy also claims that in Drieu's political choices and in his literary work there can be found a "strong current of realism."[64] An independent reading of Drieu's novels and essays certainly supports this contention, and the passage cited as an epigraph to this chapter is but one of many. In 1934 he was already sympathetic to Pan-Germanism and predicted the *anschluss*, stating that he was always in favor of "what is going to happen" (*ce qui va se faire*).[65] Soucy suggests very tellingly that part of Drieu's quest was to get away from romanticism *toward* reality.[66] In several of his writings Drieu denounced his own naive childhood romanticism as debilitating and dreamlike. Drieu stated in works such as the autobiographical novel *La Comédie de Charleroi* (1934) that the brutal reality of the First World War, which he had witnessed firsthand as a common soldier in the trenches, had killed his youthful romanticism. One can find this theme also in Drieu's drama, for example *L'Eau fraîche*, in which one of the characters chides himself for having given money to a female friend, adding: "Only with brutality can one make people happy" (*Il n'y a qu'avec de la brutalité qu'on fait le bonheur des gens*).[67]

Many other elements which in our normal vocabulary we term realist can be found in Drieu's writings, for example his frank assertion that the ends justify the means, his willingness to get his hands dirty, his detestation of ivory-tower intellectuals, "miserable little *clercs*, little monks in robes," whose agitation is merely verbal.[68] Drieu came to admire a cold, hard professionalism, as exemplified in the scene from his best-known novel, *Gilles* (1939), in which the Franquists execute republican prisoners. Drieu undoubtedly emphasized success in his political action; for example he abandoned Jacques Doriot's fascist *Parti Populaire Français* when he realized that it was not going to take hold as a major political force. Soucy argues that Drieu went almost to the point of "ideological nihilism." For Drieu it was worse to lose than to be wrong ideologically. Just before his suicide, as the Russian armies were nearing Berlin, Drieu made statements favorable to Soviet communism.[69] The hard-bitten realist element in Drieu, Soucy believes, is thus very important in explaining his conversion to fascism and his collaboration; otherwise the romantic aspects of his thought might have taken on a "relatively harmless, or even humane direction." Two of the ugly elements of fascist ideology, the acceptance of brutality and

the glorification of violence, "were palatable to Drieu less because he was an advocate of romanticism than because he was
an advocate of realism."[70]

Soucy's contentions tend to be supported by George L.
Mosse, who views Drieu as "perhaps the most interesting
French fascist." Drieu and others were looking for the
"genuine underneath the rationalizing of life," but Mosse
emphasizes, "this search for the 'genuine' was *not* supposed to
be a return to romanticism." Mosse goes on to note Drieu's
argument (made in 1939) that the decadence which he and his
fellow fascists found so prevalent in western liberal society
had come about because sentimentality had taken over the
creative drive.[71]

Julien Benda would of course agree with Soucy and Mosse,
since he believed adamantly and argued vehemently that almost all modern intellectuals, whether communists, fascists,
or supporters of some other political movement, were
realists. One of his greatest laments was that the *clercs* had become realists.[72]

Robert Brasillach—Romantic or Realist?

But what about Robert Brasillach? Perhaps he at least was as
romantic as Sérant, Vandromme, and others claim? He was of
a later generation than Drieu, and was only five years old in
1914. Thus he did not have his illusions shattered by the terrible experience of trench warfare, which as Frank Field has
shown, so deeply affected intellectuals like Drieu la
Rochelle.[73] Certainly Brasillach's end had romantic overtones; he even wrote poetry in prison while awaiting execution, consciously imitating André Chénier whose magnificent
prison poems of 1794 are viewed by critics as important early
romantic works. (Brasillach's writings were taken out by his
lawyer; Chénier's had to be smuggled out with his laundry.)

Yet the issue is not a simple one to resolve. It is curious that
in an early, and severely critical essay, Brasillach found fault
with Pierre Drieu la Rochelle for being at heart a liberal republican. Drieu's fascism, the younger man believed, was

only vocabulary, and he had no concrete, real system. Brasillach felt that Drieu was too attracted by the "demons of abstraction,"[74] and that he must finally come down to reality. *"Until the real has a part in his books*, let us turn ourselves away from his clouds and his ennuis."[75] Thus we find the supposedly romantic Brasillach accusing Drieu of lack of realism!

Is this example merely a fluke? Brasillach's *oeuvre*, after all, runs to twenty-eight volumes. It includes poetry, political journalism, history, criticism (literary, theatre and cinema), novels and autobiographical writings. The poetry, a small portion of his total work, written *in extremis*, may justifiably be viewed as romantic in theme and in tone. But what about the remainder?

Unless the meaning of the word "romantic" is distorted beyond all commonly accepted definitions so as to become virtually unrecognizable, there is no way that the political journalism, which constitutes the largest single block of his writings, can be deemed romantic. Brasillach is writing to serve a cause, and shows no humanity, no traditional moral scruples whatsoever. He demonstrates time and time again a brutal pragmatism; conciliation with his enemies would be possible, but only on his own terms, that is "by pumping lead into their vital organs and through the 'definitive and peaceful conciliation of the coffin.' "[76]

Brasillach co-authored two works of history, the first a brochure with Henri Massis, *The Cadets of the Alcazar*, romantic in the sense that it is full of praise for the noble and heroic virtues of the young cadets who held off a republican seige of the Alcazar of Toledo until a Franquist relief column could arrive during the Spanish Civil War.[77] At the same time it is pure Franquist propaganda, with no pretense at balance and objectivity, as is the full-length *Histoire de la guerre d'Espagne*, written in collaboration with Maurice Bardèche, and published in 1939 just after Franco's victory. As Brasillach and Bardèche tell the story, Franco and his associates are on the side of truth, justice, and social order, have in reality the support of the vast majority of the Spanish people and are representing their basic needs and wishes. The Popular Front coalition is portrayed as weaklings at best (Azana) or villains pure and simple (the communists). Brasillach and Bardèche are especially enthusiastic about a periodical they call *l'Action espagnole*, ideologically close to *l'Action française*. Without the "little group of lucid intellectuals, who did not fear action," associated with this periodical, Franco's revolution would never have taken place.[78] The only possibly romantic element in this lamentable "history" would be its admiration for the warlike and courageous Spanish temperament. Its basic aim is to show that the defeat of the republican forces in Spain saved the rest of Europe from international communism.[79]

On the other hand, while the literary criticism, as we have seen, contains at least some statements which are overtly realistic, Brasillach's criticism, especially for the theatre and cinema, is more romantic in tone. It is often light, airy and whimsical, sometimes acute and sensitive, and is concerned with the magic of celluloid which preserves the fleeting moment of high drama in a way that the stage cannot.[80] Brasillach could also be very serious in tone in his theatre criticism, was a passionate and knowledgeable theatregoer, who liked stage drama because it is the most "tragically human" of all the arts, and because of its dreamlike qualities.[81] In general, we may conclude that the romantic elements in Brasillach's nature served as the inspiration for his theatre and cinema criticism, though there is one curious exception when Brasillach discusses the great actor-director Louis Jouvet, stating admiringly that "Louis Jouvet never gives in to romanticism, . . ."[82]

In discussing the question of Brasillach's presumed romanticism, his novels must be considered. During his lifetime he published seven, and today is probably best known as a novelist. An examination of the content of these novels provides evidence to support contradictory interpretations. Common themes include an emphasis on youth, youthful love, a frequent lament over the inevitability of aging.[83] These could fairly be termed romantic. The horror of growing old is especially prevalent in his most popular novel, *Comme le Temps passe* (1937), which had sold 82,000 copies in paperback by 1970. René and Florence, the two chief characters, are raised in Majorca and return to Spain for their honeymoon. The first of the two key scenes in the novel is a luxuriant fourteen-page description of the sexual act, at the end of which Brasillach rhapsodizes that the process of aging is halted, "in this instant of unconquerable youth, which will belong to them for eternity, no matter what happens."[84] The final dramatic scene takes place in a Paris theatre, where the lovers meet after a long separation, and first see each other in a tarnished and blurry mirror, so that the signs of aging are invisible. Thus René and Florence enjoy another of those rare moments "when man can escape from time."[85]

On the other hand, Brasillach's novels were not always so romantic, and they manifest a remarkable elasticity and shifting of emphasis; the author was very adept at changing styles to keep up with the times. In his first novel, *Le Voleur d'étincelles*, published in 1932, the hero discovers his family roots after a visit to a cemetery. (One thinks immediately of Barrès' doctrine of *La Terre et les morts*—the Earth and the Dead—and this novel is very much in the Barrèsian mode.) Brasillach's second novel, *L'Enfant de la nuit* (1934), capitalizes on the trend toward populism found in many contemporary works, especially Jules Romains' massive serial novel, *Les Hommes de bonne volonté*, which began to appear in 1932, and reached twenty-seven volumes when it was completed in 1946. *L'Enfant de la nuit* does deal with youthful romance and the coming of age of the young hero, but it also devotes a great deal of attention to the common people of Paris, stating at the end that simple people have a real story to tell: "There are no ordinary beings" (*Il n'y a pas d'êtres ordinaires*).[86] These early, fundamentally apolitical, novels may be compared with the ardent defense of fascism in *Les Sept Couleurs* (1939), and the virulent attack on the Resistance combined with a restrained yet favorable portrayal of the Nazi occupiers in Brasillach's last novel, *Six Heures à perdre*, written in 1944 but left in manuscript until 1953.[87] My purpose here has not been to pass judgment on the literary merit of Brasillach's novels, to determine whether they were original or imitative, but simply to emphasize that they provide conflicting evidence for our consideration of the motivation behind Brasillach's commitment to fascism. To claim that his novels are fundamentally romantic is to ignore the pragmatic and realistic elements they contain.

The most important single source, more useful than his novels, for the study of Brasillach's fascist engagement, is his volume of memoirs, *Notre Avant-Guerre* (1941). Here he talks openly about his political choices and also offers some perceptive commentary on an entire intellectual generation which came of age in the late 1920s and went off to war at the end of the next decade. *Notre Avant-Guerre*, which has recently been translated into Dutch, has been seen as a significant social document.[88] With regard to the romantic versus realist question it contains evidence which on first examination appears to be contradictory. There are frequent references to a sort of anarchistic spirit and a cult of youth, which could be construed as romantic. William R. Tucker has shown persuasively that there is a strong ingredient of anarchism in Brasillach's fascism.[89] Yet does an anarchistic spirit necessarily lead to fascism? In *Notre Avant-Guerre* Brasillach describes his friends thus: "We were eighteen, we had a little spiritual confusion, rather a lot of disgust for the modern world, and a fundamental penchant toward anarchy."[90] Brasillach's sentences could just as well have categorized an exactly contemporary group, the young leftist revolutionary intellectuals in Paul Nizan's novel, *La Conspiration*.

The matter is even more complicated since Brasillach always laid great emphasis on an elite close-knit group of friends, all young, with a similar ideological outlook, which he often described as the "gang," using the English word.[91] If we review Brasillach's list of companions, we find that one of his closest friends at the time was the young surrealist Roger

Vailland, whom he greatly admired and whom he thought had anarchistic tendencies.[92] A character in *Comme le Temps passe*, the Catalan anarchist Ventura Pia, is said to be modeled after Vailland.[93] Vailland, however, moved in an opposite direction politically from his youthful associate, becoming a Resistance leader, author of what is still perhaps the finest novel on the French Resistance, *Drôle de Jeu*.[94] In 1952, Vailland joined the *PCF*, though he became disillusioned fairly quickly, and resigned after the Soviet repression in Hungary in 1956. He remained an independent leftist.[95] Thus a penchant for anarchism, whether we deem it romantic or not, can as easily lead to communism as to fascism.

Another piece of evidence from *Notre Avant-Guerre* which is difficult to evaluate is Brasillach's mention on several occasions of Claude Roy.[96] Roy, a very subtle and perceptive literary critic,[97] was born in 1915 and was a close associate of Brasillach during the late 1930s. He wrote for *l'Action française, Je suis partout*, and other right-wing journals. He was viewed as one of the rising stars in the rightist intellectual firmament, and presumably would have taken his place as an heir to Charles Maurras and eventually to Brasillach himself. However, after the fall of France Roy's political alignment diverged dramatically from that of Brasillach. He joined the Resistance *and* the Communist Party. Roy did remain a loyal enough friend to Brasillach to sign the petition asking for the commutation of the latter's death sentence, but then he changed his mind and crossed out his name.[98] In *Communism and the French Intellectuals*, David Caute discusses Claude Roy's decision to join the *PCF* and states that he did so "in a mood of exultant romanticism, his head full of John Reed's *Ten Days that Shook the World*, the novels of Malraux, the poems of Mayakovsky and Pablo Neruda."[99]

Whether or not Caute's account of the reasons for Claude Roy's joining the *PCF* is completely accurate, Roy's case does show that it is as difficult to generalize about the links between romanticism and fascism as between romanticism and communism or any other political movement. The fact that colleagues of Brasillach evolved in such different directions politically points up the impossibility of predicting the political choices of individuals, either by unearthing some presumed common quality such as anarchism or by taking any sort of generational approach. No preestablished definition of an intellectual generation will work; if there is a common denominator, it has yet to be discovered. Certainly it is not romanticism, and neither is it class or educational background. The 1920s in Paris was the time of the education of an extraordinary galaxy of brilliant intellectuals, most of whom came from the same middle-class background as did Brasillach, and all of whom had a very similar education. Many were fellow graduates of the *Ecole Normale Supérieure*. When we realize that Jean-Paul Sartre, Paul Nizan, Simone de Beauvoir, Maurice Merleau-Ponty, Simone Weil, Claude Lévi-Strauss, and Emmanuel Mounier, to name only the most eminent, were all born within a few years of Brasillach, and that all except Mounier were educated in Paris, we recognize the problematic nature of any sort of generational approach.

Thus far in our analysis of Brasillach's autobiography we have dealt only with his references to other intellectuals. It is important to note that even in speaking of himself he does not always sound romantic in *Notre Avant-Guerre*. For example, he relates that as a very young man he did not participate in student political struggles as had his friends:

> I was not sure enough of myself and of my opinions to take sides. Nonetheless, my first political reflections encountered the *Action Française* of Maurras, and from that time forth they have remained in that direction. Suddenly a world opened up [after reading Maurras], *that of reason, that of precision, that of truth*.[100]

Brasillach displays tremendous admiration for Maurras in *Notre Avant-Guerre*, calling him "that magnificent man, that prince of life," terming him the greatest thinker of his age and comparing him to Socrates.[101] Maurras (1868-1952) was a neoroyalist, a believer in *raison d'état*, and strong advocate of classicism. "He had always regarded romanticism as a foreign import which distorted the French spirit, a barbarous and confused patchwork of ideas and emotions."[102]

Certainly, then, the first important mentor whom Brasillach cites in his autobiography was no romantic, unless one unearths some residue hidden underneath half a century of vehement denials. Brasillach's worshipful attitude toward Maurras did not prevent an eventual open break between the two men over the issue of collaboration. Maurras could not tolerate Brasillach's Germanophilia, and after 1941 would have nothing to do with his former disciple.[103] Whether this quarrel marked a totally new philosophical direction for Brasillach is open to question. The issue seems to center around differing political judgments, and given the extent of German power in 1941, one might argue that Maurras had finally lost his political realism and that he, not Brasillach, was surrendering to a romantic inspiration.

In *Notre Avant-Guerre* Brasillach does refer to the group of close friends who became fascist sympathizers in the middle 1930s, after concluding that the royalism of Maurras' *Action Française* was admirable but insufficient. The members of this group were not very intellectual, Brasillach notes; in fact they denounced intellectuality. They were not persuaded of the importance of books and ideas, even if they dealt with them as their stock-in-trade, and they did not take themselves very seriously.[104] Whether such an attitude is romantic or not is again debatable.

Brasillach's reactions to a visit to the Nuremberg Party Congress in 1937 are highly admiring, and they suggest a new-found seriousness. Brasillach was fascinated by the splendid ceremonies, and especially liked the youth work camps, which showed ". . . seriousness, virility, the hard and powerful love of the fatherland, total devotion."[105] In this disciplined unity Brasillach found the strength of the new Germany, and he felt that at least some of the lessons of

Nazism must be applied to France. His trip to Nuremberg brought on a feeling of regret for what "democracy has done to France." Hitler, whom he was able to observe at close range, deeply impressed him. He admired the Führer's sense of destiny and his mystical power, finding in Germany "a surprising mythology of a new religion." France, Brasillach thought, might have had a "prefascist" spirit in the late 1930s, but he does not conclude with any definitiveness on this matter. For him and his group, he emphasizes, French fascism was not a political or an economic doctrine, nor an imitation of a foreign political system, but rather a "spirit." "It is precisely the spirit of friendship, which we would like to raise to the level of national friendship."[106] (Given Brasillach's anti-Semitism and anticommunism, "national friendship" would of course have excluded all Jews and all communists unless the latter were to adopt fascism.)

In *Les Sept Couleurs* (1939), the most openly fascist of Brasillach's novels, one of the leading characters, clearly a spokesman for Brasillach himself, elaborates upon the appeal of fascism. He speaks of the "joy" felt by the fascist, which cannot be comprehended by the "radical committee-member, the skinny judeosocialist conspirator." Whether or not fascism becomes the dominant force in the twentieth century, he feels that "nothing can prevent the joy of the fascist from having existed, and from having held sway over individuals, *both by sentiment and by reason*."[107] In a note dated November 22, 1935, the same character states: "I believe in prudence and I believe in necessity. What must be done is seize them both."[108]

While Tucker never sets down explicitly the reasons he finds for Brasillach's commitment to fascism, one can discern in his book on Brasillach what might be termed a "modified romantic" approach. Tucker strongly emphasizes Brasillach's *lack* of intellectual discipline, his lack of any real awareness of external historical realities. In an earlier article on Brasillach, he claimed that Brasillach tried sincerely to be simultaneously antibourgeois and anticommunist,[109] and never realized that "fascism was an ideological disguise of the new national imperialisms." Brasillach deluded himself into thinking that he was a standard-bearer of a universal spirit of regeneration—in actuality he was "only an adjunct of the German propaganda machine."[110] Tucker's interpretation, that Brasillach was a romantic pretending to be a realist, has a certain plausibility, but much of the evidence cited heretofore could equally well support the reverse position, that Brasillach was a realist pretending on certain occasions to be a romantic. It is arguable that there is truth in the prosecuting attorney's claim that Brasillach had sometimes been opportunistic,[111] and Tucker himself accepts this position as having plausibility.[112] We have seen that Brasillach at times in his writings sounds very realistic, very organized, very rational, and very pragmatic. One could describe him as a highly intelligent man who made certain guesses about the probable future, based on the best evidence available to him. He thought that fascism would win and so he engaged himself with the winning cause,[113] rather than offering *de facto* support to the *status quo* by abstaining from politics and remaining a "pure" intellectual.

What I am suggesting is that the best explanation for the commitment to the fascist cause made by Robert Brasillach, and quite probably by other French fascist intellectuals, is that they decided to become *engagé* and made consequent political choices because of reasoned and careful judgments that turned out to be wrong. This explanation is not completely original, in that it is quite similar to Maurice Merleau-Ponty's analysis of the reasons for collaboration in *Humanisme et terreur*, first published in 1947.[114] Merleau's interpretation does not appear to have been picked up by later scholars, probably because his discussion of collaboration is an aside, and the primary aim of his book, which has generated a lot of controversy,[115] is to offer an existential interpretation of Stalinism and of the Moscow Purge Trials.

If this interpretation of fascist engagement has validity, we would have to conclude that Brasillach at some point became fully aware of his error, a point that could have been no later than January 1943, when the Nazi defeat appeared inevitable to the observer possessed of even minimal intelligence. By January 1943, when Von Paulus capitulated at Stalingrad and the handwriting was on the wall, there were no clear options open to Brasillach. He did resign from the staff of the openly collaborationist and violently anti-Semitic newspaper *Je suis partout* in September 1943, but doubtless realized that this gesture would not be enough to clear him in the eyes of an eventual judge and prosecutor. He certainly did not view this action as romantic in inspiration; he wrote to Lucien Rebatet in August 1943, while trying to decide about resigning, "I do not wish to do anything that resembles romanticism" (*Je ne veux pas faire du romantisme*).[116]

The Decision to Face Trial

Perhaps Brasillach becomes a romantic at least after September 1943. Tucker notes that in his last days Brasillach only made passing references to the fact that he had been wrong about the war,[117] and also notes that even though he left *Je suis partout* before it became *Je suis parti* in August 1944,[118] the flow of procollaboration articles continued to the very end: "For as the military tide turned and the collaboration movement reached an impasse, he continued his journalistic acts of aggression as if to squeeze every last degree of satisfaction from his ill-fated venture. That he had not received any significant financial rewards in the process seemed to give his shamelessness a degree of purity that was all the more startling."[119] Plumyène and Lasierra suggest that in this final period (September 1943–August 1944) Brasillach "ended by losing sight of reality, and his fascism became delirium."[120]

Yet if one were a person of some courage and a certain sense of honor, however perverted, one could conceivably decide that the realistic step to take, as the Allied armies approached Paris in the summer of 1944, would *not* be to run off to Germany or to Switzerland. Both of these options, which were chosen by such fascist or fascist-sympathizing intellectuals as Louis-Ferdinand Céline, Jean-Pierre Maxence, Al-

phonse de Châteaubriant, and Lucien Rebatet, were available
to Brasillach, but he would have lived out his life in exile,
while being either totally forgotten or totally vilified in his
homeland. Brasillach went into hiding after the liberation of
Paris, but gave himself up when he learned that his mother
had been arrested. She was released. Thus he chose to face
trial and gamble. Of the four possibilities remaining to him,
the least likely, though not impossible given his eloquence
and the skill of his lawyer, would have been a sympathetic
jury and a verdict of innocent. Much more probable would
have been a long prison term and eventual amnesty, which
historically did occur. Almost 40,000 persons were imprisoned in France for collaboration; by the end of 1948 only
13,000 were still in custody; by October 1949, 8,000; by 1951,
4,000; by 1956, sixty-two; and by 1964, just twenty years
after the Liberation, not one remained in prison.[121]

The third and very strong possibility would have been the
death penalty after the trial, but a commuted sentence and
thus eventual amnesty with all the others. (The statistics cited
earlier show that only about one in three of those condemned
to death were actually executed. The odds turned out to be
even better as far as Brasillach's peers were concerned. Four of
the six intellectuals studied by Sérant in *Le Romantisme fasciste*
received death sentences, but in only one case was the sentence carried out.)[122]

Finally, if all else were to fail, one could, with an eye to
posterity and with the famous and ennobling precedent of
André Chénier firmly in mind, begin to prepare one's posthumous reputation. In writing the *Poèmes de Fresnes* while in
prison, Brasillach consciously modeled himself on Chénier,
though his poetry seems pale and maudlin when compared
with Chénier's Ode to Charlotte Corday or to *Comme un der-
nier rayon* ("As a last ray of light"), a magnificent poem probably written one or two days before he went to the guillotine.
The final couplet reads:

> *Souffre, o coeur gros de haine, affamé de justice*
> *Toi, Vertu, pleure si je meurs.*

(Suffer, heart filled with hatred, thirsting for justice
  You, Virtue, cry if I die.)

Brasillach must have been reading Chénier long before he
went to prison, for he also managed to complete a manuscript
on the martyred poet while in prison. His book on Chénier
was published after his death, in 1946.

Thus one might argue that even though Brasillach lost the
gamble for his life, he was acting quite reasonably given the
circumstances. In a sense he succeeded, as far as his posthumous reputation is concerned. Had de Gaulle followed his
original inclination and commuted the death sentence, there is
every reason to believe François Mauriac's prediction, made
in 1957, that Brasillach would eventually have joined the
forty "Immortals" in the French Academy.[123] But given the
evolution of postwar France and Europe, he probably would
have become an anachronistic crank in the manner of his
brother-in-law, Maurice Bardèche, and perhaps he would not
enjoy such great popularity, with his works reprinted in
mass-circulation paperback editions, several biographies already published including one in English, a novel based on his
trial, and a formal society, based in Lausanne, which pub-
lishes *cahiers* in his honor, and claims a membership list of fif-
teen hundred, including the late Monsignor Roncalli, who
did not resign when he became Pope John XXIII.[124]

Psychological Factors

If the preceding analysis has been persuasive, we can conclude
that for Robert Brasillach "realism" was a more important
motivation for his enduring commitment to fascism than was
"romanticism." We have seen that a persuasive case can be
made that the same holds true for Drieu la Rochelle. A rather
natural inference would be that these realistic or pragmatic
choices were made because of some special quality in the ethical or psychological makeup of the individuals concerned. In
other words, the explanation is carried a step further by as-
suming the existence of a particular trait, or set of traits, such
as the "authoritarian personality," which would be present in

all those intellectuals who took the step of opting for fascism.

Once again Robert Soucy has done brilliant and pioneering work in an essay on the "Psycho-Sexual Aspects of the Fascism of Drieu la Rochelle,"[125] but this time the comparative method seems to lead to formidable if not insuperable difficulties. These difficulties deserve brief discussion here, since they bear directly on the question of "Why fascist engagement?"

Taking Drieu la Rochelle first, we discover that he was a bitter, morose, very unhappy man, who had a miserable childhood. His father scorned him and accused him of cowardice and his mother overprotected him. There is both a great deal of brutal misogyny and a great deal of eroticism in his writings, and he was a notorious womanizer himself.[126] Soucy shows persuasively that as far as Drieu's adult sexuality was concerned, he conformed to the psychoanalytic model of the authoritarian personality almost perfectly.[127]

Brasillach, on the other hand, by all accounts had a very happy childhood, and had a rather sunny, cheerful disposition. Women are quite favorably treated in his novels; his father died when he was five and he was then surrounded by women in his immediate family until his mother remarried. His very close relationship with his sister continued after she married his friend Maurice Bardèche. I have found a number of hints and one open assertion that Brasillach was a homosexual.[128] Tucker concludes that he was probably not, though he does note the rather indelicate way Brasillach spoke of having "slept with the Germans."[129] Whether or not Brasillach was a homosexual, his personality certainly differed dramatically from Drieu's; the latter was, publicly at least, an ardent heterosexual, with two wives and countless mistresses and a real cult of maleness.[130] Whatever Brasillach's sexual preferences really were, he was in every way so different from Drieu that it is clearly impossible to generalize on the basis of personality traits. Homosexuality cannot explain a commitment to fascism any more than it can account for a dedication to antifascism.[131]

These brief comparative remarks are by no means intended to deny the validity of the psychoanalytic or psychohistorical approach to the study of fascism, but merely to point up the preliminary state of our knowledge. Detailed psychobiographies of a significant number of French fascist intellectuals, and probably antifascists to provide controls, must first be prepared. To carry out such work successfully private papers and journals must be available, and this is not always the case. Some interesting results may eventually be forthcoming. As a model we have Peter Loewenberg's important studies of Nazi leaders and movements.[132] At present it does not seem possible to generalize about personality type or unconscious factors in searching for the motivations behind a commitment to fascism. We are not yet ready to challenge Alastair Hamilton's conclusion in *The Appeal of Fascism*, that "we are less than ever entitled to say that a certain type of man, a certain type of psychology tended toward fascism."[133]

THE RIGHT TO ERROR

> It is one of the fundamental tenets of American Democracy that intellectual error is innocent.
>   Christian Gauss[134]

When Robert Brasillach decided not to go to Switzerland or to accept the German offer of asylum made in the summer of 1944, he set in motion a chain of events which led to his execution. We have attempted to show that an element of realism was involved in this decision. In normal usage, a "realistic" choice may involve a certain gamble, but it must be a gamble based on the possibilities for action which seem available in a given historical context, rather than bravura, foolhardiness, or some romantic notion. There is good evidence that from the point of view of continuing literary reputation, Brasillach won his gamble. In a second sense he gained a victory, in that there was a substantial debate at the time of his trial over the justice of the proceedings and of the sentence. This debate found its way into the press and had widespread echoes and an important influence on the intellectual climate of the immediate postwar years.[135]

At the outset of any discussion of the justice of the sentence imposed upon Brasillach, one point should be made clear. If Brasillach had been fully consistent with his own fascist doctrines, he would have accepted the death penalty, even without the pretense of a trial, as deserved. In his journalism he frequently called for the death of his enemies. Before the fall of France he at least advocated a trial first; after 1941, summary execution—and as for the Jews, the children should be sent to concentration camps along with the adults.[136] In the novel *Les Sept Couleurs* there is a passage which praises the new *uomo (sic) fascista*.[137] Such men ". . . do not believe in a form of justice which emanates from words, but they call for that justice which reigns by force."

On the other hand, fifty-nine eminent French intellectuals felt that Brasillach should have been reprieved. (It is interesting that their petition mentions nothing about Brasillach's professional background or deeds, but merely asks for clemency because his father "died for the fatherland on 13 November 1914.") The list includes men of undisputed distinction, several of whom were or would become Nobel Prize winners and members of the French Academy. Among the signers were François Mauriac, Paul Valéry, Paul Claudel, Georges Duhamel, the Duc de Broglie, Jacques Copeau, Jean Paulhan, Vlaminck, Derain, Honneger, Jean Anouilh, and Albert Camus.[138]

In the debate stirred up by the petition for clemency for Brasillach, one of the arguments put forth most frequently by his defenders was that intellectuals deserve a special sort of immunity. This has been phrased as the "right to error," and relates so closely to the question of freedom of speech that the issues may be inextricable. The doctrine of the "right to error" seems often to get special emphasis in periods of historical crisis, when intellectuals as a class are under attack. The passage by Christian Gauss cited above dates from a time when Senator Joseph McCarthy's power and influence were on the rise in this country.

With the passing of Julien Benda,[139] it would be difficult, if not impossible, to find an intellectual or professor in this country or in Western Europe who would be willing to give up the "right to error." Surely it is one of our most cherished intellectual freedoms, a freedom that writers and artists strive to attain in countries where it is unavailable. Yet does this mean that all intellectuals would support clemency for someone like Brasillach? Perhaps not, even today, for two reasons. The first is trivial, and unworthy of the calling of intellectual, but who would dare deny its very real existence? It is the simple fact that many of us insist on the "right to error" for ourselves, but are reluctant or unwilling to grant it to others.

The second reason is more substantial and worthy of consideration, and relates to the problem of how to separate out error from the consequences of error. Does the right persist when we can demonstrate that its practice has led to the death of others?[140] In a collection of memoirs of Resistance leaders published in 1970, René Tavernier, who had edited *Confluence* from Lyon during the Occupation, recalled a "bad moment" when he read in *Je suis partout* an article by Brasillach denouncing the influence of resisters, Jews, and Anglophiles in a number of publications based in the southern zone, including his own. Tavernier stated that "my first reaction was not anger against Brasillach, but fear." He added that he thought he would be arrested at any moment, and therefore took new precautions. Brasillach's condemnation was thus just, according to Tavernier, because "writing in a journal during the war that a certain publication is a den of Jews and resisters, equals a death sentence for them. If the Gestapo never did arrive, that simply proves that the Germans did not read *Je suis partout* attentively, that they did not take Brasillach seriously."[141]

René Etiemble took a somewhat similar position in an article published in 1952, reacting to the news of Maurice Bardèche's release from a term in prison.[142] Etiemble stressed that he was not among those who lamented Brasillach's death, noting that as early as 1943 he had stated and published (in clandestine and exile journals, of course), that he hoped Brasillach would face a firing squad. "I find quite odious the hagiographic publications in which his memory is celebrated, stained as it is with Jewish blood."[143] To be sure, Etiemble did not want Brasillach to be a scapegoat and pay for the crimes of others, and he regretted that the economic and political collaborators had not always received just punishments. Etiemble does not give a clear indication as to how he would stand on the "right to error" issue, but he does stress the utter repulsion and horror he felt for fascist intellectuals like Brasillach and Bardèche. Their crime, he states, is compounded because they were intelligent; they did not have "the excuse of Laubreaux [who wrote for the racist paper *Gringoire*]: stupidity."[144]

Thus for René Etiemble, Brasillach was not only a political enemy but a common criminal, guilty of murder. His assertion that Brasillach was more guilty because he possessed intelligence implies that intellectuals have a special responsibility because of their unique skills and privileged position in society. During the 1960s, this notion was taken up and elaborated upon by Noam Chomsky and others in America, primarily in response to the Vietnam War and specifically reacting to the role "establishment intellectuals" were playing in that conflict.[145] If one agrees that intellectuals do have special responsibilities and that they also possess a "right to error," one would conclude that the "right to error" must stand in a very intricate, possibly dialectical, relationship to a duty, an obligation to society.

The defense lawyer at Brasillach's trial asked the rhetorical question, "Do civilized peoples execute their poets?" In a very perceptive analysis of the trial, Herbert Southworth suggests that this question is "humiliating for poets, since it places them in a special category, like irresponsible children. Brasillach was executed for collaboration with the enemy. The condemnation was probably a political error, for it made a myth out of Brasillach, which if he had lived, would have been erased by time itself and by his own political naiveté."[146] Both Brasillach's enemies and his defenders would agree with Southworth that an error of political justice was made, though his enemies would add that the error was understandable, given the conditions in liberated France during the winter of 1944-1945.

However, there will most likely never be agreement on the absolute or moral justice of Robert Brasillach's trial and sentence. On every major anniversary of his execution, the issue resurfaces in France. On February 6, 1975, a young historian, Pascal Ory, reviewed the whole Brasillach case in *Le Monde*, including a balanced discussion of Brasillach's deeds and works, of the romanticism versus realism question, and of the "right to error" controversy.[147] In his conclusion, Pascal Ory notes that had he been thirty years older he could have served in the Free French Charlemagne Division, and that while on February 6, 1975, he is prepared to sign an appeal in favor of the abolition of the death penalty, on February 6, 1945, "in the name of a certain idea of the intellectual and of the militant, I would accept to be included among the twelve men who executed at dawn the condemned man, Robert Brasillach. . . ."[148] Needless to say Ory's article inspired a large number of heated letters to the editor, some passionately defending his position, others attacking it.[149] Because the life and death of Robert Brasillach raise all the great questions connected with intellectual engagement, we may expect that the debate over the case of this fascist intellectual will continue as long as there exists an identifiable social grouping with a sense of separateness which can be termed the "intellectual class."[150]

V

◊◊◊◊◊◊◊◊◊

Conclusions: Why Engagement?

◊◊◊◊◊◊◊◊◊

An artist worth his salt is permanently separated
from ordinary reality. On the other hand, we all
know that the constant unrealness of his innermost
being will sometimes fill him with despair, and that
he will then attempt what is strictly forbidden him,
to trespass upon actuality. . . .

Nietzsche[1]

Why do artists, poets, professors and others who are usually
classified as "intellectuals" leave the ivory tower and "trespass upon actuality?" What prompts them to abandon their
normally sedentary ways and descend into the arena? The
question is not a new one. Matthew Arnold tried to come to
grips with it in *Culture and Anarchy*, published in 1869.[2]
Nietzsche, of course, had his own ideas on the subject.

We have thus far dealt with this question only as it relates to
the special case of fascist intellectuals. The fascist variant of
intellectual engagement died with the burst of gunfire that
took Robert Brasillach's life and with Pierre Drieu la Rochelle's suicide a month later. Barring some extraordinary
reversal, inconceivable to this writer, no revival is possible
from that quarter. What about the motivation behind the more
common types of engagement? We recall that leftist intellectuals created and elaborated upon the concept of engagement—from Rolland and Barbusse in the early 1920s, who
if they did not use the concept of engagement understood
the issues surrounding it—to Nizan, Mounier, Sartre,
and Julien Benda himself, that *clerc de gauche*. During the

Dreyfus Affair and again after the mid-thirties Benda was indisputably *engagé*.

Can we derive a general theory that will be applicable to most cases of engagement, that is when the conscious and willful choice to enter the arena is based upon principles which may be broadly defined as "leftist"? (An ideal-typical listing of these principles would include humanitarianism, antielitism, some variant of socialism or at least a concern for social justice, pacifism or antimilitarism, and internationalism.)

Various explanations for leftist engagement have been offered, and as one would expect they are sharply colored by political bias. Those who find leftist engagement blameworthy argue that the "eggheads" are ignorant idealists who meddle in what is not their business, suffer from a hidden (perhaps unconscious) resentment of those who hold political office, and in reality lust for power themselves.[3] An anarchist motivation, apparently illogical when linked to a desire for political power, may also be present,[4] and a few would go as far as to find diabolical inspiration. Some variant of these views on the causes of political involvement of leftist or liberal intellectuals is shared by many politicians, businessmen, and others active in the "real" world, and often by conservative intellectuals, who may or may not admit their own involvement.

Though there are exceptions,[5] the consensus is that when leftist intellectuals choose to become *engagé*, their primary motivation is not to produce an immediately discernible historical effect. Most would agree with Jean-Marie Domenach that "the intellectual has the right to be impotent."[6] Those who have openly defended engagement from a leftist point of view have tended to follow Emmanuel Mounier in arguing that there is a moral root to their actions. Their engagement provides an ethical ingredient in political life which otherwise would be lacking. Since it is nearly impossible to separate out the effect of their political involvement from the ebb and flow of broader historical events such as wars and revolutions, the most they could hope for would be that their engagement provided some check upon the greed and ambition of their rulers. Perhaps, as in the case of intellectual protests against a war or colonial policies, engagement might trigger a positive reaction in the larger society.

With varying degrees of elegance, vehemence, and persuasiveness, the question of "Why engagement?" has been argued back and forth by the French intellectuals studied in this book and by many others.[7] No one denies that the phenomenon of engagement exists, and that it has significance. Whether that significance is beneficial is another matter.

There does seem to be one common ground among almost all the disputants, namely that some form of sociological definition of the intellectual should serve as a starting point; i.e., the intellectual class is defined according to the social function it performs. A distinction is made between what intellectuals regularly do and the workaday activities of the rest of humanity.

It may, however, be enlightening to ignore, or at least set aside, social function while examining the motivation behind the political involvement of intellectuals. This novel approach was first suggested by the late J. P. Nettl in a posthumously published essay, "Ideas, Intellectuals, and Structures of Dissent." Nettl is perhaps best known for his biography of Rosa Luxemburg. His tragic death in a plane crash in the fall of 1968 cut short a brilliant career.

Nettl leads into the problem of "Why engagement?" by first dealing with definitions. He is critical both of Julien Benda's idealistic insistence on a sharp distinction between men of action and *clercs*, and of the traditional sociological teaching, which has defined intellectuals according to their social role (thus agreeing with Benda, though for different reasons and arguing from different basic premises). The sociological approach is exemplified in the writings of such distinguished scholars as Talcott Parsons and Edward Shils.[8] With Parsons and Shils, Nettl writes, "the focus is thus on role definition and contrast with other roles, often by analogy; the result, an emphasis on the free and unattached nature of intellectuals as a social role which entirely ignores the very attached or *engagé* nature of the ideas they articulate."[9]

Nettl proposes to view the question of what constitutes an intellectual from the angle of types of ideas rather than types of men. The basic distinction he draws is between ideas of scope and ideas of quality. "Scope" ideas refer essentially to university work, to scientific and technical knowledge and to much of the cultural patrimony which is taught to new generations of students in university classrooms. Ideas of "quality," on the other hand, while they may not shift as dramatically with new discoveries, involve some sort of preferential restructuring and some form of qualitative dissent. This second form of thought is therefore more political and ideological. Thus, according to Nettl, "scope" ideas will flourish in the institutionalized university, whereas "quality" usually pertains to intellectual production outside the university. Marx, of course, fits well into this scheme as one whose ideas of qualitative dissent were better fitted to "socio-political diffusion" than to "academic transmission."[10] Thus, following Nettl's definition, Marx was an intellectual and Hegel was not.

Nettl makes the provocative observation that only very recently have universities become places where ideas of *both* scope and quality have been articulated. That is to say, intellectuals have only recently entered the universities, since for Nettl the true intellectual has a "relationship to socio-political dissent, at least potentially."[11] Nettl elaborates on this point by arguing that the ideas of the true intellectual "must be predicated on the assumption that they are capable of being put into effect in society." They must be universal in dimension, concerned with the "quality of life *in general*."[12] Thus one cannot equate the intellectual with any traditional profession; clusters of intellectuals might well shift in social and economic grouping through time, while in a world without conflict there would be no intellectuals, even though there would be new ideas. A clear inference from Nettl's analysis is that true intellectuals must automatically be *engagé*, by the very nature of the ideas they deal with.

Nettl selects France during the Third Republic as the turning point of a new development. It was there, he believes, that qualitative dissent gained its first foothold in the universities. It is striking that in this analysis by a British scholar writing in the United States about an international phenomenon we are drawn back to France, where we have located the roots of engagement. In this theoretical essay Nettl does not attempt to document his assertion that qualitative dissent actually reached "up" into the universities during the Third Republic. Paul Nizan would have disagreed with regard to the faculties, though one wonders whether all the teaching could have been done by watchdogs. As far as the students are concerned, the activities of such individuals as Robert Brasillach, Emmanuel Mounier, Claude Lévi-Strauss, Simone de Beauvoir, Jean-Paul Sartre, Simone Weil, and Paul Nizan himself offer some preliminary verification of Nettl's hypothesis. Every one of these intellectuals went through the French university system in the late 1920s, and common sense suggests that at least some of the classroom mentors of this brilliant and diversely engaged group must have fit Nettl's category of "intellectuals."

To be sure, throughout most of the history of higher education, the academic or mandarin, the "fully institutionalized," professors have controlled the universities.[13] It is they who according to Nettl have the primary task of diffusing ideas of scope to students, "without any predicate of social action."[14] Nettl is careful never to deny the social value, indeed the necessity, of the academic mode of thought, though he does not hide his personal preference for intellectuals. He never indicates whether he views himself as an intellectual or as an academic. Within the educated classes, those who deal primarily with ideas of scope are naturally more numerous and powerful, while the presence of even a limited number of "true" intellectuals in a university system would lead to an explosive situation, since "mandarins and intellectuals live uneasily together and dislike each other intensely."[15] Nettl's insight here is remarkable, and suggests new ways of understanding many of the bitter conflicts within American universities during the 1964-1971 period (and quite possibly in their European counterparts, too). When Nettl died, the agitation throughout the universities of the world had not yet reached its peak, though he predicted that it would probably decline.[16] If one accepts Nettl's dichotomy, one might argue that as college and university administrators, the natural allies of the mandarins, began to regain their shattered confidence and take hold of the situation after 1971, efforts were renewed to drive out the intellectuals.

Nettl's view of the future of those who deal with ideas of qualitative dissent was not optimistic. At best the dominant academics will view the dissenting intellectual as a fool and helpless; "he is left to bay at the moon."[17] Nettl predicted that intellectuals would become more and more isolated as the very growth of universities pushed them toward a scope orientation in their teaching and learning. There is always the possibility of some form of "institutionalized dissent" emerging from within the universities, but Nettl was not very hopeful.[18] All the evidence available to him as he wrote his essay in the summer of 1968 (just after the French student rebellion in May), suggested that modern society "inhibits the existence of intellectuals."[19]

In the first chapter we have emphasized the necessity of the ingredient of group involvement before engagement in its modern sense becomes possible, and Nettl lays heavy stress on his conviction that intellectuals must form into groups if they are to realize their identity. The intellectual seeks to "structure himself in a crevice of disagreement," and may find himself "sliding helplessly down a glass-smooth surface, crying but not gripping. . . ."[20] Solitary dissent is not adequate; dissenters need a "suitable social structure to fulfill the role of intellectuals. . . ."[21] In his conclusions Nettl does admit that "for therapeutic reasons, if nothing else, personal dissent, however socially ineffective and unstructured, is better than none."[22]

Nettl's untimely death prevented any further explication

and defense of his fascinating theory. It surely merits critical discussion, which Nettl would have welcomed, both by those who accept the appellation "academic," and by those who have the temerity (or possibly arrogance) to call themselves "intellectuals."

A crucial implication which emerges from Nettl's theory is that a kind of identity or symbiotic relationship exists between the intellectual and engagement. We recall that when a group with a conscious self-identity, calling itself by a new name, *les intellectuels*, emerged in France during the Dreyfus Affair, it did so in order to take a political stance, to work for the Dreyfusist cause.

Ideas do appear rather hard to control, though it is evident that strenuous efforts have been made in the past to do so. Few would deny that such efforts will continue in the future. Still, one might infer from Nettl's analysis, in spite of his personal pessimism, that the appearance of intellectuals (and thus the manifestation of engagement, of critical dissent), is not just a passing phenomenon, born on the streets of Paris in 1898 and dying there exactly seventy years later. Doubtless Nettl is correct in asserting that the emergence of intellectuals (in organized groups, at least), is "only an occasional phenomenon in history."[23]

The crux of the question hinges on whether we agree with Nettl that some of the ideas intellectuals regularly confront in the quietude of their studies and libraries exert a kind of internal pressure driving them toward engagement. This argument is remarkably similar to Paul Nizan's claim that true culture has a directly revolutionary significance, and that the attainment of true culture has an explosive effect and leads to the will to transform society. If Nettl and Nizan are correct, there is a small possibility that the volatile situation in the universities throughout the world in the late 1960s did not simply represent the final surge of an outdated and nostalgic engagement by intellectuals,[24] resisting the pressure of the mandarinate on the one hand and the hedonistic, apolitical elements in the youth culture on the other. That time of upheaval might be predictive of future developments.

Epilogue: A Note on
Jean-Paul Sartre

◊◊◊◊◊◊◊◊◊

When one wishes to get rid of a great man, one
buries him under flowers. But what to do if he refuses burial?[1]

Of the three intellectuals most responsible for creating,
elaborating, and popularizing the concept of engagement,
two, Nizan and Mounier, are long dead, though their influence persists and may indeed be growing.[2] The third, Jean-
Paul Sartre, has shown no desire to become an institution,
and has struggled to retain his independence, even to the
point of refusing the Nobel Prize. Despite his best efforts, he
has probably become the most famous intellectual in the
world. His own voluminous writings have been carefully collected by Michel Contat and Michel Rybalka,[3] and he is the
subject of countless articles, dissertations, and books.[4]

Sartre has never fled from polemic and, since 1945, from
political action.[5] With the possible exception of Alexander
Solzhenitzyn, it is difficult, in 1978, to think of a more controversial living intellectual. To make any judgment of
Sartre's many ventures into the political arena would be beyond the scope of this study, and an extremely hazardous undertaking. Sartre represents a classic case of the problem of
standards, discussed in Chapter I in relation to *embrigadement*.
One may detect an irony here, in that there most probably
will never be agreement as to whether Sartre's efforts to
realize the concept of engagement in his own life have been
even partially successful. For many, his ventures into the
political arena deserve condemnation, if not for their arrogance, intolerance and error, then because they appear, on the
surface at least, to have been ineffectual. In the opinion of one
of his admirers, he has continued to struggle for a third of a
century, "... against Nazism, against racism, against all op-

pression. A combat, ever doubtful, dialectical, at the same time for engagement in history and against alienation in a faith."[6] The author of these words, Dominique Desanti, would appear to speak from personal experience, as she was one of the most militant Stalinist apologists in the 1950s before breaking with the French Communist Party.[7]

Sartre has at least tried to face the full consequences of his beliefs, and persistently risked imprisonment by accepting the nominal editorship of a series of extreme left periodicals in the early 1970s. Finally he came under the indictment he willfully sought.[8] He admitted rather ruefully that he would most likely never actually be imprisoned.[9] He continues to live austerely, and has given away a goodly portion of his substantial income to leftist causes and writers. As late as 1972 he had an unremitting scorn for hesitant intellectuals who refused to take the step into real (i.e., illegal) action.[10] In an extremely candid interview on the occasion of his seventieth birthday, Sartre has discussed his future plans, now that the onset of near total blindness has made creative philosophical and literary work impossible.[11]

As is widely known, Sartre has shifted political positions many times, in response to external events and perhaps also to keep his politics in line with his own evolving philosophy, which is now most often described as existential Marxism.[12] Particularly in the complex and controversial area of his shifting relationship to the French Communist Party and the world communist movement, Sartre has made a number of errors of political judgment, which he has admitted with a frankness rather unusual for an intellectual or an academic.[13] Without trying to determine whether Sartre's political involvement ever approached "true" engagement, one may agree with Raymond Barillon that Sartre's actions deserve to be taken seriously. "One refuses to laugh at a man who engages himself at the very age when many are borne toward the sweet philosophy of 'comprehension,' of forgetfulness, and of indifference toward what tomorrow will be the pain of others."[14]

Notes

◇◇◇◇◇◇◇◇◇

PREFACE

[1] The matter of definition will be examined more carefully in Chapter I. For convenience and consistency the noun "engagement" and the verb "to engage" will not be italicized, whereas the adjective "*engagé*," which betrays its French origins, will be in italics throughout.

[2] Preface to Roger Martin du Gard, *Oeuvres complètes*, I (Paris, 1955), p. xvii.

[3] For full documentation, see my *Roger Martin du Gard: The Novelist and History* (Ithaca, 1967), Chap. VI, "The Dilemma of Political Involvement."

[4] Cf. Clément Borgal, *Roger Martin du Gard*, 1st and 2nd eds. (Paris, 1957 and 1963), Chap. I, "Incognito." This is the standard biography in French, and in future editions Borgal will take into account the material I discovered (letter to the author from Borgal, September 15, 1967).

[5] "A fine project, but so vast, needing such sensitive treatment" (letter to the author from Pierre Chambat, May 30, 1976; Chambat's elegant phrase loses much in translation).

[6] See Jack Newfield, *A Prophetic Minority* (New York, 1967), p. 15, and Paul Jacobs and Saul Landau, *The New Radicals* (New York, 1966), pp. 9, 322-33.

[7] Written in 1969 and published in *French Historical Studies*, Vol. VII (Fall 1971). Part of Chapter I was delivered as a lecture at the University of Iowa in March 1975. Chapter III is a revised version of an article which appeared in the *Journal of the History of Ideas*, Vol. XXIV (January-March 1973). Chapter V, in an abbreviated form, was first published in the *Journal of Social History*, Vol. VIII (Winter 1974).

[8] The title of an interesting sociological study by Charles Kadushin (Boston, 1974). Kadushin believes that the true intellectual elite in this country was not heavily *engagé* in the 1960s, and in the 1970s may become more alienated and withdrawn (pp. 355-56).

[9] See Chapter V for some tentative thoughts on this question.

[10] See Chapter III.

[11] I chose 1920 rather than 1927, when Julien Benda published *La Trahison des clercs*, because the earlier date marks the founding of the French Communist Party, with all that implied for intellectuals in politics. The decade of the 1920s serves basically as a prelude to engagement. Engagement becomes a significant reality in the 1930s,

and therefore the central focus of this book is on the first half of the time span so tellingly described by H. Stuart Hughes as that of "The Obstructed Path" (*The Obstructed Path. French Social Thought in the Years of Desperation 1930-1960*. New York, 1968).

CHAPTER I

[1] *Confessions of a Disloyal European* (New York, 1969), p. 201.

[2] To cite a few examples among many, the lead article of the *New York Sunday Times* travel section for June 6, 1971, is entitled: "We have met the 'Enemy' and found them Human—*Tourisme Engagé*." In the *New York Times Book Review* (July 15, 1973), p. 1, "politically engagé" is used to characterize the British critic Raymond Williams. The word appears also in *Newsweek*, January 20, 1974, p. 41, in an article discussing the Breton language independence movement; and finally in two references to André Malraux, in *Time Magazine*, November 15, 1971, p. 40, and the *New York Times*, November 24, 1976, p. 64.

[3] Sartre and Nizan will be discussed briefly later in this chapter, Mounier in more detail. All three were of the same intellectual generation, all in fact born in 1905. On Nizan, see also Chapter III, and on Sartre, the Epilogue.

[4] Manuèle Wasserman has shown persuasively that the French romantic artists, especially the poet Lamartine, were the "precursors of the many French twentieth-century engaged artists including the Existentialists" (*Artists in Politics in Nineteenth-Century France*, unpublished Ph.D. thesis, Department of History, Columbia University, 1977, p. 5).

[5] The significance of the Dreyfus Affair has been emphasized by countless historians and sociologists, perhaps never more forcefully than by Hannah Arendt in *The Origins of Totalitarianism* (New York, 1951).

[6] *Histoire politique de la revue "Esprit" 1930-1950* (Paris, 1975), p. 9.

[7] *La Jeunesse d'un clerc* (Paris, 1936), p. 205.

[8] See Victor Brombert, *The Intellectual Hero* (Philadelphia, 1960), pp. 21-24. Also, Louis Bodin, *Les Intellectuels* (Paris, 1964), pp. 5-9. In a recent essay, William M. Johnston corrects the work of Brombert and others by showing that the essayist and novelist Henry Bérenger (1876-1952) was using *intellectuel* in a systematic way as early as 1890 ("The Origin of the Term 'Intellectuals' in French Novels and Essays of the 1890's," *Journal of European Studies*, Vol. 4, 1974, pp. 43-56).

[9] *Prisoners of Honor. The Dreyfus Affair* (New York, 1973), p. 197.

[10] "Engagement tegen wil en dank: Franse intellectuelen en de Dreyfus-affaire," *Tijdschrift voor Geschiedenis*, Vol. 87, No. 3 (1974),

pp. 410-24. The entire issue is dedicated to the theme of "Ge-schiedenis en Engagement"—History and Engagement. It is interest-ing that the Dutch have also borrowed the term from the French. See note 39.

[11] *L'Affaire Dreyfus*, 4th ed. (Paris, 1968), p. 7. Jaurès should have been excluded from this list since he was primarily a political figure. Perhaps Anatole France could have been substituted.

[12] *Ibid.*, p. 8.

[13] Another example of when intellectual engagement seems to have had a traceable political influence is discussed in Chapter II, and the question will be reexamined in Chapter V. Pierre Miquel does seem to represent a minority view. The more common opinion has been eloquently stated by Jean-Marie Domenach in an article prob-ing the weaknesses of contemporary French society: "The intellec-tual has the right to be impotent. Not the government" (*Le Monde hebdomadaire*, November 13-19, 1969, p. 7).

[14] Bodin, *Les Intellectuels*, pp. 20-21.

[15] The bibliography is enormous. Among the more useful surveys in English are Daniel Aaron, *Writers on the Left* (New York, 1961); Richard Crossman, ed., *The God that Failed* (New York, 1950); Alas-tair Hamilton, *The Appeal of Fascism* (New York, 1971); Neal Wood, *Communism and the British Intellectuals* (New York, 1959); David Caute, *Communism and the French Intellectuals* (New York, 1964); and Donald Fleming and Bernard Bailyn, eds., *The Intellectual Migration* (Cambridge, Mass., 1969).

[16] "English Intellectuals and Politics in the 1930's," in Philip Rieff, ed., *On Intellectuals* (New York, 1969), pp. 228-29. The bibliogra-phy on intellectuals in Spain is extensive. A good general study from the anti-Franquist point of view is Herbert R. Southworth, *Le Mythe de la croisade de Franco* (Paris, 1964). For a fascinating account of how a monarchist, anti-Semitic, Catholic intellectual shifted under pres-sure of events, see Georges Bernanos, *Les Grandes Cimetières sous la lune* (Paris, 1938), esp. p. 237. Bernanos made his famous protest "to unburden my soul" (*pour délivrer mon âme*). See also Antoine de Saint-Exupéry's moving portrayal of why one man, a bookkeeper, joined the republican cause (*A Sense of Life*, Adrienne Foulke, tr., New York, 1965, pp. 119-23).

[17] See Chapter IV.

[18] From *Les Lettres françaises* (September 9, 1944). Reprinted in J. Plumyène and R. Lasierra, *Les Fascismes français. 1923-1963* (Paris, 1963), p. 189.

[19] In Jacques Debû-Bridel, ed., *La Résistance intellectuelle* (Paris, 1970), p. 98. This whole collection is most useful. Another very per-ceptive analysis of the special kind of freedom the Resistance offered

the intellectual was made by the former surrealist Roger Vailland. The intellectual felt none of the usual societal obligations; he was no longer a *salarié*. See Vailland's autobiographical novel, *Drôle de Jeu* (Paris, 1945), esp. pp. 20-29, 288-89, 303, 370. *Drôle de Jeu*, translated into English in 1948 as *Playing for Keeps*, is a little-known classic of Resistance literature.

[20] Cited in Candide Moix, *La Pensée d'Emmanuel Mounier* (Paris, 1960), p. 190.

[21] *Commitment in Modern French Literature* (London, 1967), p. 38. Adereth's vigorous defense of the political involvement of the writer is subtitled "A Brief Study of 'Littérature Engagée' in the Works of Péguy, Aragon, and Sartre." Cf. also Herbert Lüthy, "The French Intellectuals," in George B. de Huszar, ed., *The Intellectuals* (Glencoe, Ill., 1960), p. 445: "The phrase, 'Littérature engagée,' was created by the writers and journalists of the Resistance who for a few years dominated the literary and political scene; and it was finally degraded into the catchword of a clique."

[22] *Paul Nizan: Committed Literature in a Conspiratorial World* (Princeton, 1972), pp. 202-15.

[23] Review of *Nizan*, by Ariel Ginsbourg, in the *Romanic Review*, Vol. LVIII, No. 4 (December 1967), p. 311. Cf. Redfern, *op. cit.*, p. 209: "Sartre often betrays green envy toward Nizan, as if he imagines him as an improved alter ego."

[24] Adereth, *op. cit.*, p. 26.

[25] Paul Nizan, *Les Chiens de garde*, 2nd ed. (Paris, 1965), pp. 49, 23, 43.

[26] Reprinted in the collection entitled *Au-dessus de la Mêlée* (Paris, 1915), p. 8. I am indebted to Joan Kalikman for this reference.

[27] Emile Poulat, *Naissance des prêtres-ouvriers* (Paris, 1965), esp. pp. 228, 326, 385, 413. Often "engagement" would appear several times in a single paragraph of the worker-priests' writings. Perhaps the most fascinating illustration comes from a priest's defense of the continuing value of his religion in the midst of the chaos and violence of World War II. "Why, after a [concentration] camp in which a few true Christians had borne witness with a revolutionary engagement, with a love and a faith as immense as God and Humanity, did eight nonbelievers come to ask from me, in maladroit and imprecise terms, the *sacrement of engagement*, baptism?" (cited in Poulat, p. 409, italics mine). See also my review article of Poulat's masterful study of the worker-priests, "Birth of a Movement," *Journal of Social History*, Vol. 4, No. 1 (Fall 1970), pp. 88-94.

[28] Moix, *La Pensée d'Emmanuel Mounier*, p. 164.

[29] Emmanuel Mounier, *Le Personnalisme* (Paris, 1949), p. 111n.

[30] Georg Lukacs, a Hungarian who usually wrote in German, has

been suggested as another source by George Steiner. Steiner argues that "Sartre's concept of *engagement* . . . derives largely from Lukacs" (preface to Georg Lukacs, *Realism in Our Time*, J. and N. Mander, trs., New York, 1964, p. 8). Though Lukacs' influence has been an extremely important and often overlooked factor in twentieth-century European intellectual history, there appears to be no evidence to support this particular claim. See, for example, Lucien Goldmann, "Introduction aux premiers écrits de Georges Lukacs," *Les Temps modernes*, No. 195 (August 1962), pp. 156-90.

³¹ See Emile Bréhier and Paul Ricoeur, *Histoire de la philosophie allemande*, 3rd ed. (Paris, 1954), pp. 197-209.

³² Manfred G. Frings, *Max Scheler* (Pittsburgh, 1965), p. 21.

³³ John Raphael Staude, *Max Scheler, 1874-1928* (New York, 1967), p. 245n.

³⁴ This bibliographical information is from Bréhier and Ricoeur, *op. cit.*, pp. 229ff.

³⁵ (Paris, 1949; an exact reprinting of the 1930 edition), p. 117. See also the discussion of Scheler's philosophy of religion, which is defined on p. 125 as a "phenomenology of religion," with emphasis on the particular intentional act, in this case the religious act.

³⁶ "L'Acte philosophique de Max Scheler," *Recherches philosophiques*, Vol. VI (1936-1937), pp. 299-312. Scheler's philosophical importance is stressed, and he had, Landsberg claims, a sense of being in the world. Landsberg feels that the intellectual danger for Scheler was a "certain chaotism," rather than the nihilism which was Nietzsche's weakness: "Scheler risks losing himself in the plenitude of his encounters" (p. 300).

³⁷ No. 62 (November 1937), pp. 179-97.

³⁸ See Charles F. Wallraff, *Karl Jaspers. An Introduction to His Philosophy* (Princeton, 1970), pp. 5-8, and 215-19. Also Bréhier and Ricoeur, *op. cit.*, p. 229. There is an interesting direct linkage between Jaspers and Sartre and Nizan in that the two Frenchmen, while students in their early twenties, collaborated on a revision of the translation, by Kastler and Mendrousse, of *Psychopathologie générale* (Paris, 1928). See Redfern, *Paul Nizan*, p. 223.

³⁹ See Dieter Ehlers, *Technik und Moral einer Verschwörüng: 20. juli 1944* (Frankfurt and Bonn, 1964), *passim*. Ehlers studies the techniques used by the organizers of the July 20 attempt against Hitler, and discusses the moral implications of these techniques. The French word *engagement* is used in the German text to denote the moral commitment of these men. (I am grateful to Professor Hsi-Huey Liang for this reference.) See also note 10 above.

⁴⁰ *Survey*, No. 91/92 (Spring/Summer 1974), pp. 121-59.

⁴¹ The letter was first published in *l'Art libre*, Brussels, February

1922. Reprinted in *Textes politiques, sociaux et philosophiques choisis*, Jean Albertini, ed. (Paris, 1970), p. 215. (I am grateful to Professor David James Fisher for pointing out this source to me.)

[42] *Ibid.*

[43] Of the other three references, the most striking is found in Rolland's open letter of March 1922, "To his Communist friends," which concluded his contribution to the debate with Barbusse. Rolland argues for Liberty of the Spirit and against the stubborn narrowness of many neophyte Marxists, adding ". . . if I am lost in a forest and am shown a single road which manifestly leads into a swamp, am I obliged to engage myself upon that road, under the pretext that I don't know any others? It is precisely because I know that this path [i.e., the rigid Marxist path] is not at all a good one that I reject it; and wisdom counsels me to search patiently for another route" (*ibid.*, p. 232). The key French passage reads, . . . *si j'étais égaré dans un forêt et que l'on m'indiquât une seule route qui manifestement menât à une fondrière, serais-je tenu de m'y engager, sous prétexte que je n'en connais pas d'autre?*

[44] "Réflexions," *NRF* (February 1931), pp. 247-54.

[45] Reprinted in *Littérature engagée* (Paris, 1950), p. 15.

[46] Gide never did join the *AEAR*, nor the Communist Party, though by 1934 both his friends and his enemies were convinced that he had taken the full step into party membership. The whole episode of Gide's involvement during the 1930s is most fascinating, and has been widely studied. See especially Caute, *Communism and the French Intellectuals*, pp. 237-41; Georges Brachfeld, *André Gide and the Communist Temptation* (Geneva, 1959); and Jean-Pierre Bernard, *Le Parti Communiste Français et la question littéraire* (Grenoble, 1972), pp. 153-76.

[47] Month of publication given in Jacqueline Leiner, *Le Destin littéraire de Paul Nizan* (Paris, 1970), p. 110. The book had been circulated and read by July 1932, since André Gide discussed it in his correspondence with Roger Martin du Gard and in a journal notation dated July 19, 1932 (André Gide, *Journal, 1889-1939*. Paris, 1951, p. 1133).

[48] See note 8 above.

[49] See the chapter "Des Années tournantes," in Jean-Louis Loubet del Bayle, *Les Non-Conformistes des Années 30* (Paris, 1969), pp. 11-31.

[50] L. Bodin and J. Touchard, *Front Populaire 1936* (Paris, 1961), p. 15.

[51] *La Politique des partis sous la IIIe République*, 3rd ed. (Paris, n.d.), pp. 318-19.

[52] Ariel Ginsbourg, *Nizan* (Paris, 1966), p. 3.

[53] Jean-Albert Bédé, review cited in note 23 above, p. 312.

[54] Nizan, *Les Chiens de garde*, p. 61.

[55] *Ibid.*, p. 70.

[56] *Ibid.*, pp. 26, 71, 96, and 40.

[57] In a 1935 review Nizan argued that the creative artist must take the risk of getting involved in action: "If one does not engage himself in action, one will merely write novels that fail, hearsay novels." His hope was to find for the writer "an alternating rhythm between action and creation which would allow him to pass from engagement in politics to a story about politics." Reprinted in Paul Nizan, *Pour une Nouvelle Culture*, Susan Suleiman, ed. (Paris, 1971), p. 174.

[58] Paul Nizan, *Le Cheval de Troie* (Paris, 1935), p. 237. (The French reads "cette lourdeur des engagements qui comporte la mort.")

[59] *Ibid.*, p. 80.

[60] See Paul Nizan, "Sur un certain front unique," reprinted in Suleiman, *Pour une Nouvelle Culture*, pp. 51-65 (first published January 1933). This is one of Nizan's most vehement attacks on the *Esprit* group, and he does not hesitate to link the personalists closely to Hitler. Mounier to be sure never went in that direction, but on his rather close relationship to the Pétain government in its early period, which he later disavowed, see J. W. Hellman, "Emmanuel Mounier: A Catholic Revolutionary at Vichy," *Journal of Contemporary History*, Vol. 8, No. 4 (October 1973), pp. 3-23. See also, Chapter III, note 75.

[61] *Esprit*, No. 4 (January 1933), p. 669. This brief involvement with an extreme right political movement is perhaps not surprising for the great-great grandson of a royalist executed by the republicans during the French Revolution. Nizan's first biographer, Ginsbourg, believes that Nizan joined the Camelots du Roy, the youth wing of the Action Française, in 1924, just before he entered the Ecole Normale Supérieure (Ginsbourg, *Nizan*, p. 7). See also Leiner, *Le Destin littéraire de Paul Nizan*, p. 29, who claims that Nizan's youthful right-wing engagement was with that curious native French fascist movement, Georges Valois's *faisceau*. On Valois, see Jules Levey, "Georges Valois and the Faisceau: The Making and Breaking of a Fascist," *French Historical Studies*, Vol. VIII, No. 2 (Fall 1973), pp. 279-304.

[62] *Les Non-Conformistes des années 30*, esp. pp. 29-31, for Loubet del Bayle's discussion of the "will to renewal" (*volonté de renouvellement*), and pp. 126-77.

[63] *Esprit*, No. 1, p. 22 (the French is *qui nous engageons*). Sometimes in these first issues Mounier uses *engagé* and *engagement* in an older sense, e.g., pp. 34, 38, and especially p. 129, where it is noted

that the publishing of a common statement for the personalist movement "does not engage them [the contributors to *Esprit*] at all."

[64] First citation from the first issue of *Esprit*, p. 23, the second from No. 6, March 1933, p. 873.

[65] *Esprit*, No. 1, p. 23.

[66] Mounier, "Certitude de Notre Jeunesse," *Esprit*, No. 8 (May 1933),

[67] Cited in Lucien Guissard, *Emmanuel Mounier* (Paris, 1962), p. 28.

[68] See Jean-Paul Sartre, *Qu'est-ce que la littérature?* (Paris, 1948), p. 26, the discussion of the "sector of unpredictability" in man, despite the tremendous conditioning each individual undergoes. For Sartre, this is liberty, and "man is nothing else but his liberty." Or, the statement from a 1966 interview, "The Essential is not what one has done to man, but *what man does with what one has done to him.*" (*Arc*, No. 30, 1966, p. 95. Italics his.) To be sure Sartre never acknowledged any debt to Mounier.

[69] *Esprit*, No. 8 (May 1933), pp. 233-34.

[70] See *Les Chiens de garde*, p. 17.

[71] *Esprit*, No. 8 (May 1933), p. 234.

[72] For a discussion of *témoin* and *témoignage*, terms commonly employed to describe the social function of contemporary French writers, see my *Roger Martin du Gard* (Ithaca, 1967), pp. 14-16. At the end of the sixteenth issue of *Esprit*, there is a fascinating example of Mounier's effort, not always successful, to separate engagement from *témoignage*. A copy of a petition to the French government is attached, an early example of the kind of statements that will be familiar to readers of the *New York Times* during America's involvement in Vietnam. The petition is a protest against colonialist repression in Indochina. A full investigation is demanded, amnesty for those arrested, and at the minimum Mounier insists that some rights be granted to the colonies as they move toward autonomy. The petition is introduced as follows: "The duty of everyone in a barbaric world is to bear witness and engage himself everywhere evil breaks out" (*de témoigner et de s'engager partout où sévit le mal*).

[73] Cf. Winock, *Histoire politique de la revue "Esprit*," p. 7. Winock finds the political aspects of *Esprit* particularly revealing ". . . of the permanent tension intimately lived by the intellectual between the will to *témoignage* and the will to efficacity."

[74] Mounier, *Le Personnalisme*, p. 111.

[75] Guissard, *Emmanuel Mounier*, p. 15.

[76] Irresponsible in the sense of placing too much emphasis on the "I"—what Mounier was criticizing as early as 1932.

[77] Preface to *Portrait de l'aventurier*, 2nd ed. (Paris, 1965), p. 22.

[78] *Ibid.*, p. 24.

[79] Stéphane, *Portrait de l'aventurier*, p. 104.

[80] *Time Magazine*, November 15, 1971, p. 40.

[81] Bodin, *Les Intellectuels*, p. 79.

[82] Landsberg, "Réflexions sur l'engagement personnel," p. 180.

[83] Samuels, "English Intellectuals and Politics in the 1930's," p. 221.

[84] Moix, *La Pensée d'Emmanuel Mounier*, p. 328.

[85] *Ibid.*, p. 22. See also pp. 51-52, the discussion of the *dégagement* that for Mounier always followed engagement.

[86] *Ibid.*, p. 329.

[87] "The Intellectual as a Social Role Category," in Rieff, *On Intellectuals*, pp. 4-5, 21. One exception to the usual definition is found in Kurt H. Wolff's provocative essay, "The Intellectual: Between Culture and Politics," *International Journal of Contemporary Sociology*, Vol. 8, No. 1 (January 1971), pp. 13-34.

[88] According to this definition, Paul Nizan himself was frequently *embrigadé* during the 1930s. In commenting on his talents as a literary critic, his biographer Jacqueline Leiner writes, ". . . in spite of his engagement [we would prefer *embrigadement* in this context], which too often led him to praise or condemn writers according to their more or less pronounced adhesion to Marxist doctrine, Nizan demonstrated on many occasions a subtle penetration of spirit which makes us forget the political propagandist" (*Le Destin littéraire de Paul Nizan*, p. 214).

[89] Victor Brombert in *The Intellectual Hero* traces the development of that sense in France, and Raymond Williams in his classic *Culture and Society* (New York, 1958), admirably details the rather similar striving for identity among nineteenth-century British intellectuals.

[90] See Chapter v.

CHAPTER II

[1] *The Opium of the Intellectuals*, Terence Kilmartin, tr. (New York, 1962), p. 302 (published in French in 1955).

[2] "Subjective Si! Objective No!," *New York Times Book Review* (April 5, 1970), p. 36.

[3] Michel Winock, *Histoire politique de la revue "Esprit" 1930-1950* (Paris, 1975), p. 10.

[4] The most famous defense of the Dreyfusard intellectuals is Charles Péguy's poignant memoir, *Notre Jeunesse* (Paris, 1910), while the protofascist writer Maurice Barrès characterized the supporters of Dreyfus as more guilty than the Captain himself. "Those

who are really responsible, who ought to be punished, are the 'intellectuals,' the 'platform anarchists' (*les anarchistes de l'estrade*), the 'metaphysicians of sociology.' A prideful band of fools. People who show a criminal complaisance in their intellect, who treat our generals as idiots, our social institutions as absurd, and our traditions as unhealthy" (*Scènes de doctrines du nationalisme*, Paris, 1902, p. 208). Another early denunciation of the intellectuals, by a former anarchist turned supporter of Charles Maurras' *Action Française*, is Edouard Berth, *Les Méfaits des intellectuels* (Paris, 1914).

[5] Eliot wrote an early, perceptive, and quite favorable review of *The Treason of the Intellectuals* in the *New Republic* (December 12, 1928), pp. 105-7. A more recent example would be Lewis Coser's essay, "Julien Benda—On 'Intellectual Treason,' " *Encounter* (April 1973), pp. 32-36. Coser writes, "We have been neglecting Benda at our own peril and are badly in need of antidotes against the 'with it' intellectuals, the Sartres, Marcuses and Mailers of the age" (p. 34). Other commentators will be cited in this chapter. For a full bibliography see Pierre Chambat, *Julien Benda, 1867-1956* (University of Paris Doctoral Thesis in Political Science, Paris, 1976), Vol. IV. Chambat's thesis is a complete bio-bibliographical study and far surpasses all previous work on Julien Benda. I am grateful to Chambat for allowing me to use a prepublication copy of his thesis.

[6] Professor André Lwoff remarks on how badly misunderstood Benda has been in his own country, citing the "anonymous fool" who in the Larousse Encyclopedia, doubtless the sole source for knowledge about Julien Benda for many French-speaking people, defined *La Trahison des clercs* as a "pamphlet against the intellectuals" (introduction to the 1975 edition of *La Trahison des clercs*, p. 17).

[7] *The New Radicalism in America, 1889-1963: The Intellectual as a Social Type* (New York, 1965), p. xvi.

[8] H. Malcolm Macdonald, ed., *The Intellectual in Politics* (Austin, 1966), p. 9. The phrase is not a direct quote but rather was intended by Macdonald to synthesize the thrust of Benda's thesis (personal communication from Macdonald, February 27, 1970).

[9] *Ibid.*, p. 22.

[10] *Ibid.*, pp. 93, 96, 100. There is a real irony here, given Benda's fanatical hatred of Germany and all things German. See note 51.

[11] *Ibid.*, p. 120.

[12] Andrea Hellering, "The Dump Johnson Movement, 1967-1968," unpublished Senior Thesis, Vassar College, Poughkeepsie, N.Y., 1976, pp. 32-36. Hellering, who was able to interview a number of the participants, has written the best available study of this fascinating coalition of politicians, students, and intellectuals.

[13] "The Ninnyversity?," *New York Review of Books* (January 28, 1971), p. 28.

[14] "If an Artist Wants to be Serious and Respected *and* Rich, Famous and Popular, He is Suffering from Cultural Schizophrenia," *New York Times Magazine* (September 26, 1971), p. 89.

[15] "A History of Grim Frivolities," *National Review* (April 13, 1973), p. 426.

[16] "The Politics of Intransigence," *Times Literary Supplement* (January 23, 1976), p. 71.

[17] René Etiemble, "Avant-Propos," to Julien Benda, *La Trahison des clercs* (Paris, 1958), pp. i-ii.

[18] Lwoff, "Introduction," pp. 9, 17.

[19] Chambat, *Julien Benda*, Vol. III, p. 850.

[20] Aron, *The Opium of the Intellectuals*, p. 301. Despite the implications of his title, taking off as it does on Marx's attack on religion as the "opiate of the masses," Raymond Aron is far more critical of fellow travelers than of fully engaged communist intellectuals (see Preface, p. xi). Though Aron does not refer specifically to *La Trahison des clercs* until page 300 of a 324-page work, and then rather critically, one could argue that he has Benda in mind throughout. Aron chooses to bring up the earlier work on political involvement of intellectuals precisely when he is ready to give his own conclusions on the justification for that involvement. These are given on pp. 301-303.

[21] *Ibid.*, p. 210.

[22] Chambat, Vol. II, pp. 443-44 and *passim*.

[23] *Julien Benda* (Ann Arbor, 1956), p. 170.

[24] *Ibid.*

[25] Benda was always fascinated by history, wrote about it extensively, and received his *licence ès-lettres* in 1894 in that subject. André Lwoff believes that Benda possessed "the erudition of the historian" ("Introduction," p. 22).

[26] Chambat, Vol. II, p. 459, cites Niess favorably, and on this topic does not deviate from Niess' account.

[27] Niess, *op. cit.*, pp. 145-46.

[28] *Ibid.*, p. 144.

[29] *Ibid.*, p. 153. Cf. also p. 173: The book ". . . forces every intellectual to examine his conscience. . . . Its great merit is that it recalls and recalls mercilessly that the intellectual life is a true clericature, a career in which there must be no compromise with the obligations of the order."

[30] *Ibid.*, p. 301.

[31] H. Stuart Hughes, *Consciousness and Society* (New York, 1958), p. 418. The other two works chosen by Hughes are Thomas Mann's *The Magic Mountain* and Karl Mannheim's *Ideology and Utopia*.

[32] *Ibid.*

[33] *Ibid.*, pp. 411, 415-18.

[34] Benda, *Trahison*, pp. 105-6 (pagination from the third, 1958, French edition).

[35] *Ibid.*, p. 108.

[36] *Ibid.*, p. 128.

[37] It is clear that Benda, despite his own predilections, believes that intellectual activity can have significant political effect—at least the actions of traitorous *clercs*. Pierre Chambat argues that all of Benda's work is haunted by "the question of the power of the word of [true or non-betraying] intellectuals" (Vol. II, p. 533).

[38] Benda, *Trahison*, p. 129.

[39] *Ibid.*, pp. 131-32, 135.

[40] *Ibid.*, p. 135.

[41] *Ibid.*, pp. 225-26. Cf. Alan Cassels' discussion of the Italian intellectuals and fascism. Cassels notes that early in Mussolini's career as dictator, even Benedetto Croce in a series of interviews "communicated his conviction that Fascism was necessary and compatible with liberal principles, and as Croce decided, so did a great many of the Italian intelligentsia. In Italy, as elsewhere, 'the betrayal of the intellectuals,' to use Julien Benda's trenchant phrase, anteceded the death of liberal politics" (*Fascist Italy*, New York, 1968, pp. 34-35).

[42] The French *clercs* who did not protest Mussolini's brutal actions, arguing instead that too much annoyance of their southern neighbor might risk war, infuriated Benda. They should have vigorously denounced Mussolini's imperial adventures in the name of universal principles and let the diplomats worry about the practical consequences. "The treason of the *clercs* is that today they are turning themselves into ministers of foreign affairs" (Julien Benda, *Précision*, Paris, 1937, p. 28). See also Benda's introduction to the 1947 edition of *Trahison* (Paris, 1958), pp. 26-29.

[43] Chambat, *Julien Benda*, Vol. I, p. 66 and again on p. 67.

[44] Paul Nizan, review of *La Jeunesse d'un clerc*, the first volume of Benda's autobiography. Published in *L'Humanité*, January 14, 1937, and reprinted in *Pour une Nouvelle Culture*, Susan Suleiman, ed. (Paris, 1971), p. 238.

It seems clear that Benda's subjective sense of what was morally wrong and right led him to become involved in a given issue. How he derived that sense, whether it was indeed linked to eternal values or was specific and localized, is another question. Pierre Chambat suggests that a certain element of self-interest was present in Benda's political decisions; e.g., his own self-preservation, the preservation of his race, and the preservation of a country that had protected him and nurtured him, and whose culture he shared and loved passionately. Benda perhaps would have conceded this point, though always insisting on the presence of "the eternal" in his choices.

[45] Benda, *Trahison*, pp. 146-47.

[46] *Ibid.*, p. 140.

[47] This section of Benda's argument is especially prone to challenge. In order to strengthen his point that the late nineteenth century marks a qualitative change, he feels obliged to assert that political passions were foreign to the great *clercs* of the past, even Voltaire and Montesquieu, and that such nineteenth-century figures as de Maistre, Chateaubriand, and Michelet exercised their politics ". . . with a generality of sentiment, an attachment to abstract views, which properly excludes the name of passion" (*ibid.*, p. 142).

[48] Because of his role in the Dreyfus Affair and his concern with social justice, Péguy has appealed to the Left. At the same time his intense patriotism and his heartfelt, though unconsummated, longing to return to the Catholic Church, have made him attractive to the Right. Sorel (1847-1922) is a very complicated figure who made dramatic intellectual shifts throughout his career. At the end of his life he managed to admire both Mussolini and Lenin.

[49] *Ibid.*, p. 171.

[50] Benda believed that France was the last bulwark of civilization in the twentieth century, and advocated French as the language of a united Europe. Even readers sympathetic to Benda may find his arguments somewhat specious in this area.

[51] In 1949, Benda stated, "The Middle Ages had the Plague, the Twentieth Century has the Germans" (cited in Chambat, *Julien Benda*, Vol. III, p. 870). Benda believed in moral races, and was convinced that the Germans were barbarians, could never be charitable, could never create a true democracy. Yet he always claimed that he was not a racist (*ibid.*, p. 886).

[52] Benda, *Trahison*, p. 154.

[53] *Ibid.*, p. 185. (Benda was proud of his Jewish origins, but did not practice the Jewish faith.)

[54] *Ibid.*, p. 197.

[55] *Ibid.*, p. 201.

[56] *Ibid.*, p. 203.

[57] *Ibid.*, p. 205.

[58] *Ibid.*, pp. 226-27.

[59] Both the similarities and the differences in the basic philosophies of Chomsky and Benda deserve further study. Cf. especially Chomsky's famous article on "The Responsibility of Intellectuals," which first appeared in 1967 in the *New York Review of Books* and has been reprinted in *American Power and the New Mandarins* (New York, 1969).

[60] Benda, *Trahison*, p. 261. The *clercs* are as bourgeois as their masters. They attack classical studies because the classics emphasize

man's generality; they have a thirst for sensation, a need for certainty.

[61] *Ibid.*, p. 271.

[62] *Ibid.*, p. 275.

[63] See Jean-Paul Sartre's discussion of this new awareness in *Situations*, II (Paris, 1948), pp. 242 and *passim*.

[64] Benda, *Trahison*, p. 279. Benda here rejects the mystical pacifism of a Romain Rolland because of his conviction that the Germans were responsible for the First World War. Benda claims that in Rolland's case the "*mystique* of peace" has triumphed over the "sentiment of justice."

[65] *Ibid.*, p. 283.

[66] *Ibid.*, pp. 286-91. The word "civilization" is purposely not used here, since Benda is critical of the idea that one can predict any continuation of civilization. What we have been granted thus far may have been a "happy accident," since humanity has enjoyed only eleven centuries of Hellenism, then suffered through twelve centuries of the Dark Ages, and there have been only four centuries since the Renaissance.

[67] *Ibid.*, p. 294.

[68] Hughes, *Consciousness and Society*, p. 417.

[69] *Précision*, p. 7.

[70] *Ibid.*, p. 9. Benda's misogyny is undeniable, and merits a separate study. He frequently denounced Bergsonism for its "feminine sensibility" and part of his attack on romanticism, especially German romanticism, was directed against the "feminine" qualities he thought it possessed. He once wrote, "Man can think of himself without woman; she cannot think of herself without man" (from *Le Rapport d'Uriel*, cited in Chambat, *Julien Benda*, Vol. II, p. 600. This passage was cited by Simone de Beauvoir in *The Second Sex* as a typical example of sexist ideology). When he reached his early eighties, Benda did finally marry. He also claimed that he had always been in favor of female emancipation, "but because of justice, not *galanterie*" (Benda, *La Jeunesse d'un clerc*, p. 19).

[71] Benda, *Précision*, p. 19.

[72] *Ibid.*

[73] See Chapter I, note 15, for a listing of general works on the subject. An interesting recent study which concentrates on three intellectuals who became deeply engaged in the 1930s is Frank Field, *Three French Writers and the Great War* (New York, 1975). Field deals with Henri Barbusse, Pierre Drieu la Rochelle, and Georges Bernanos.

[74] Chambat entitles his admirably balanced and superbly documented treatment of this aspect of Benda's career "Le Compagnon de route" (*Julien Benda*, Vol. III, pp. 711-850).

[75] Benda, *Précision*, p. 23. He therefore approves of Zola's *J'Accuse*, but not of Anatole France's advising the Combes ministry (1902-1905). In a perceptive review of Benda's autobiography, Paul Nizan pointed out that Benda could be very insightful in tracing the sources of his personal intellectual development—namely, Greco-Roman culture, mathematical studies, and the Dreyfus Affair. "This has created a man totally engaged in a certain temporal adventure. Is it necessary to speak of eternity?" Benda has defended with the same "eternal" ardor the Ethiopians against Mussolini, and the Spanish republicans against fascism. "He will say that it is always Dreyfus that he defends in the name of the same values. . . . May I be permitted to disbelieve this claim entirely. J. Benda changes eternities, although he will not allow himself to believe it" (Nizan, review of *La Jeunesse d'un clerc*, in *Pour une Nouvelle Culture*, p. 238).

[76] Benda, *Précision*, p. 28. Italics his.

[77] *Ibid.*, p. 29.

[78] The title of Nizan's review of *Précision*, originally published in *L'Humanité*, August 14, 1937, reprinted in *Pour une Nouvelle Culture*, pp. 275-79. There is ample evidence, including Benda's own words and deeds, to confirm Nizan's assertion that Benda was "a very passionate man of the Left who has taken up the mantle of the *clerc*" (p. 276). What is debatable is whether that mantle was a protection, the quality that gave Benda his claim to greatness, or a hindrance, a straitjacket.

[79] Benda, *Précision*, p. 23. The *mystique-politique* terminology is borrowed from Benda's friend-turned-enemy, Charles Péguy, who first used it in *Notre Jeunesse* (1910).

[80] Benda, *Précision*, p. 97.

[81] *Ibid.*, p. 97.

[82] *Ibid.*, p. 99.

[83] *Ibid.*

[84] *Ibid.*, p. 149.

[85] *Ibid.*, p. 150.

[86] *Ibid.*, p. 151.

[87] The question of the degree of Benda's idealism is a difficult one and I cannot attempt to resolve it here. He certainly adhered to universal ideals and in that sense he was an idealist. On the other hand, one of his ideals was Reason and he was also a rationalist. André Lwoff points out that Marxists often haughtily dismiss as idealist conceptions which displease them, "when in fact they are simply rationalist, which the Marxists are not, while pretending to be, . . ." (Lwoff, "Introduction," p. 18).

[88] Chambat, *Julien Benda*, Vol. III, p. 741.

[89] Though Benda was to have nothing but scorn for existentialism when it gained notoriety after the war.

[90] Benda, *Précision*, p. 164. In 1947, Benda repeated this statement almost verbatim, "Questions du communisme," *Confluences* (January-February 1947), p. 48. Cf. Chambat, *Julien Benda*, Vol. III, p. 823 and *passim*. Chambat remarks frequently on the extraordinary quality of consistency in Benda, in that Benda would often lift long passages written ten, twenty, even forty years earlier and incorporate them into a new work.

[91] "Anticommunisme et Patriotisme," *NRF* (August 1938), p. 307.

[92] "Les heures graves. Un suicide," *L'Ordre* (September 1, 1939), p. 1. Cited in Chambat, *Julien Benda*, Vol. III, pp. 784-85. Benda, the *clerc* who stated that the *clerc* must never tie himself down to a regular newspaper column, contributed frequently to *L'Ordre*—77 articles from when he began submitting them in June 1938 until the last, hopeful, contribution written when the French army was defeated and the Germans almost in Paris, "Ne comptons pas trop sur l'histoire," June 7, 1940. Benda began to write for *L'Ordre* again in June 1945, and this was just one of the many periodicals to which he submitted material.

[93] From *Je suis partout*, No. 373 (January 14, 1938), p. 8. See also the savage attacks on Benda in Brasillach's collection of reviews *Les Quatre Jeudis* (Paris, 1951, reprint of 1944 edition). Brasillach finds Benda so vile and so depraved that he doesn't even deserve execution. Brasillach wrote in 1936, "the day when power in France is placed in sufficiently strong hands [i.e., a fascist dictatorship] we shall demand for Benda the benefit of the sole pitiful and just law which can be applied to him: the Gramont law [pertaining to the caging of wild animals]." From a review of *La Jeunesse d'un clerc*, reprinted in *Les Quatre Jeudis*, p. 241.

[94] Chambat, *Julien Benda*, Vol. IV, pp. 3-4.

[95] *Ibid.*, Vol. III, p. 786.

[96] See above, notes 43, 44, and 75.

[97] W. D. Redfern, *Paul Nizan: Committed Literature in a Conspiratorial World* (Princeton, 1972), p. 83.

[98] Benda, *Les Cahiers d'un clerc* (Paris, 1950), p. 120.

[99] Benda must have meant an unquestioning obedience of party directives, and an acceptance of the Marxist philosophy of history and society. At the time Benda was cooperating with the French Communist Party on many issues.

[100] Benda, Introduction to the 1947 edition of *Trahison*, p. 76.

[101] *Ibid.*, pp. 69-70. See Chapter IV for a discussion of the case of Robert Brasillach.

[102] Benda, Introduction to the 1947 edition of *Trahison*, p. 61.

[103] *Ibid.*, p. 45.

[104] *Ibid.*, p. 61. Italics his.

[105] *Ibid.*, p. 76.

[106] "Avant-Propos" to the 1958 edition of *Trahison*, p. xvi.

[107] *Ibid.*, pp. xx–xxi.

[108] On the response of the French intellectuals to the Algerian crisis, see Michel-Antoine Burnier, *Les Existentialistes et la politique* (Paris, 1966), pp. 131–46.

[109] The term "Establishment Intellectuals" appears to have been first used by Lewis Feuer in an article in the *New York Times Magazine* (March 26, 1967), pp. 22ff.

[110] "Alienated Intellectual Elite" is another convenient term coined by Lewis Feuer, and is the title of the article cited in note 109.

[111] Published by W. W. Norton. An earlier (1955) paperback edition, brought out by Beacon Press under the title of *The Betrayal of the Intellectuals*, is now out of print.

[112] The first three volumes of his memoirs, covering through the end of the Second World War, was published by Gallimard in a single volume in 1968, with an introduction by René Etiemble. In 1970 *La France byzantine ou le triomphe de la littérature pure*, first published in 1946, was reprinted by l'Union Générale d'Editions. As far as works about Julien Benda are concerned, in addition to the increasing flow of articles and shorter studies, all documented in Chambat's bibliography, there is Chambat's monumental thesis itself. It will be published as are all French theses for the *Doctorat d'Etat*. When published it will immediately replace Robert J. Niess' 1956 book as the definitive treatment of Julien Benda's life and *oeuvre*.

[113] "Introduction," p. 9. Lwoff argues that Julien Benda is one of the few philosophers "whom scientists can recognize as one of their own" (*ibid.*, p. 23). Lwoff's eloquent defense of Benda, whom he believes to be a "very great thinker" (*ibid.*, p. 10), should go a long way toward introducing Benda to a new generation in France.

CHAPTER III

[1] *Journal, 1889-1939* (Paris, 1951), p. 1138. Note of July 19, 1932. Italics his.

[2] *Julien Benda* (Ann Arbor, 1956), p. 29. See also p. 168 and *passim* on Benda's love of polemic.

[3] Cf. W. D. Redfern, *Paul Nizan: Committed Literature in a Conspiratorial World* (Princeton, 1972), p. 37. In *Les Chiens de garde* Nizan was "arguing from a position antithetical to that of Benda in his *Trahison des clercs*, . . ."

[4] Paul Nizan, *Les Chiens de garde* (Paris, 1965), p. 70. This edition will be used for all quotations from *Les Chiens de garde*.

⁵ See H. Stuart Hughes, *Consciousness and Society* (New York, 1958), Chap. II, "The Decade of the 1890's: The Revolt against Positivism." For a useful brief treatment of Bergson, see *ibid.*, pp. 113-25.

⁶ Nizan, *Les Chiens de garde*, p. 47. The source of Julien Benda's claim that he would have killed Bergson in a moment of rage is *La Jeunesse d'un clerc* (Paris, 1936), p. 201. Other enemies that he would have similarly disposed of include Emperor William II of Germany, General Mercier (from the Dreyfus Affair), Mussolini, and Charles Maurras.

⁷ See Julien Benda, *Précision* (Paris, 1937), p. 148.

⁸ See Redfern, *Paul Nizan*, pp. 84-86.

⁹ Both reviews are reprinted in Paul Nizan, *Pour une Nouvelle Culture*, Susan Suleiman, ed. (Paris, 1971), pp. 235-39, 275-79. This excellent collection of articles published between 1930 and 1939 shows both the range and the depth of Nizan's powers as a critic.

¹⁰ The text of this statement, originally published in *Le Figaro littéraire*, March 29, 1947, is reprinted in its entirety in J.-J. Brochier's biographical introduction to *Paul Nizan, Intellectuel communiste, écrits et correspondance, 1926-1940* (Paris, 1967), pp. 15-16. Among the other signers were Raymond Aron, Simone de Beauvior, Albert Camus, François Mauriac, and Maurice Merleau-Ponty.

¹¹ See Chapter II, note 111.

¹² Suleiman, Preface to *Pour une Nouvelle Culture*, p. 18.

¹³ Jean-Paul Sartre, Review of *La Conspiration*, in *Situations*, I (Paris, 1947), p. 26.

¹⁴ The Sartre preface is included in the English edition, published by the Monthly Review Press. Sartre modestly claimed in his preface that he was not responsible for the resurgence of interest in Nizan, that young people had rediscovered him for themselves, and found him appropriate to their concerns (pp. 15-16, and *passim*). Though Sartre's great prestige doubtless helped his friend's cause, Nizan's message in and of itself seems to have had a special appropriateness for the 1960s. It did not take long for its implications to be seen. During the Algerian War, before most of his works were reprinted, a clandestine revolutionary group supporting Algerian independence called itself the "Paul Nizan Group." See Ariel Ginsbourg, *Nizan* (Paris, 1966), p. 105. American critics were generally quite favorable, though they were not as certain as Sartre that Nizan was really speaking to contemporary youth, who suffer from less "fear of betrayal," or do not have the history he is talking about "at their fingertips." Cf. Guy Davenport, review of *Aden Arabie, New York Times Book Review* (June 30, 1968), p. 10, and Neal Acherson, "High on Guilt," *New York Review of Books* (August 1, 1968), p. 20.

[15] The 1966 biography, by Ariel Ginsbourg, was actually no. 84 in the twentieth-century classics series, twenty-three non-French writers having been included up to that time. One may find it ironic that no volume in this series has yet been dedicated to Julien Benda, who always proclaimed himself a resolute defender of classicism. The 1967 collection, edited by Brochier, is essential to Nizan studies. It was published by François Maspero, the courageous and independent publisher, whose own case provides a fascinating study in French cultural history. Maspero was truly an *engagé* intellectual, always willing to risk his entire venture to bring out a new revolutionary work or to reprint an old one. As of 1974 he had been indicted forty-eight times, a record in France, sixteen of his books had been banned, and he had paid many fines. During the Algerian War, when he brought out works like Frantz Fanon's *Les Damnés de la terre* (*The Wretched of the Earth*), his shop was bombed by supporters of the OAS (the secret army organization that fought a last-ditch struggle to keep Algeria French territory). Ironically, what finally forced him to close *La Joie de Lire*, his famous bookshop, was thievery by student "radicals" in the early 1970s (see Jean-Claude Guillebaud, "François Maspero menacé de faillite," *Le Monde*, December 19, 1973). In 1970, Maspero re-edited *Paul Nizan, Intellectuel communiste* in two volumes, including the same material and adding a series of nine fascinating articles that Nizan wrote in 1936 on the Spanish Civil War. Maspero also reprinted *Aden Arabie, Les Chiens de garde*, and *Les Matérialistes de l'Antiquité*.

[16] *Le Cheval de Troie* (1935) was published in London in 1937 as *The Trojan Horse*, but there appears to be no translation of the far more important *La Conspiration*. One is badly needed.

[17] *Romanic Review*, Vol. 59, no. 4 (December 1968), pp. 278-95.

[18] In addition to the Suleiman volume cited in note 9 above, see especially Jacqueline Leiner, *Le Destin littéraire de Paul Nizan* (Paris, 1970).

[19] *Aden Arabie*, 1968 (paperback edition, 1970), *The Watchdogs*, 1972, and *Antoine Bloyé*, 1973. The Redfern volume is cited in note 3 above.

[20] See Barbara Probst Solomon's review of *Antoine Bloyé* in the *New York Times Book Review* (June 23, 1973), pp. 4-5, and Karl Miller, "Episodes in the Class War," *New York Review of Books* (November 15, 1973), pp. 25-28.

[21] The Leiner and Redfern volumes are the best critical studies. Nizan's unusually forceful style, his effortless mastery of the writer's craft, have been widely noted. Cf. Sartre's review of *La Conspiration*, first published in 1938, and reprinted in *Situations*, I (Paris, 1947), pp. 26-30.

22 Sartre, "Avant-Propos," p. 10.

23 See especially David Caute, *Communism and the French Intellectuals* (New York, 1964); A. Rossi (pseud. for A. Tasca), *Physiologie du Parti Communiste* (Paris, 1948); Ginsbourg, *op. cit.*, pp. 84-106, Brochier, introd. to Nizan, *Intellectuel communiste*, pp. 14-17, and Redfern, *op. cit.*, pp. 198-209.

24 The one exception among Nizan scholars is Redfern, *op. cit.*, p. 192, who points out that it may take "more courage to divorce an illusion than to espouse one."

25 Paul Nizan, *La Conspiration* (Paris, 1968), p. 207.

26 *Ibid.*, p. 210.

27 Redfern, *op. cit.*, p. 81.

28 *Ibid.*, p. 26. Redfern argues persuasively that given Nizan's undisputed brilliance and leadership qualities he would have become a prominent and wealthy businessman had he chosen that route. Redfern also shows by citing Nizan's letters that he was much more tempted by Besse's offer than he later admitted.

29 Nizan, *Aden Arabie*, pp. 125-35, 159, 162-63, 185-87.

30 *Ibid.*, p. 79.

31 Sartre, "Avant-Propos," pp. 20-23.

32 Redfern, *Paul Nizan*, p. 22.

33 Nizan, *Aden Arabie*, p. 77.

34 Prior to the publication of Clara Malraux's memoirs, the standard account of the Malrauxs' first trip to the Far East was Walter G. Langlois, *André Malraux: The Indochina Adventure* (New York, 1966). See also Clara Malraux, *Le Bruit de nos pas*, 5 vols. (Paris, 1963-76). Volumes II and III deal with the 1920s, and Langlois had access only to Volume II.

35 Nizan, "Correspondance d'Aden," in *Intellectuel communiste*, p. 75.

36 *Ibid.*, p. 84. By 1933, in *Antoine Bloyé*, Nizan became sharply critical of a social system which places a bright child whose father is a "respectful worker" in technical school. Such a man can rise to the lower middle class, but can never become a true member of the bourgeoisie, *"un homme bien,"* who can slide a few classical citations into his conversation. Members of the lower middle class will not have the same "passwords and slogans" (*mots de passe et de ralliement*) (*Antoine Bloyé*, orig. ed. [Paris, 1933], p. 47).

37 Nizan, *Intellectuel communiste*, p. 87.

38 *Ibid.*, p. 91.

39 *Ibid.*, p. 94. Letter of February 20, 1927.

40 An especially interesting comparison could be made with the case of André Malraux, who was by all accounts apolitical and an elitist, when he was arrested during his first trip to Indochina for "stealing" Khmer statuary.

[41] Nizan, *Aden Arabie*, p. 69.

[42] Ginsbourg, *op. cit.*, p. 22.

[43] Nizan, *Les Matérialistes de l'Antiquité* (Paris, 1968), p. 15. All citations from this work are taken from the 1968 edition, the second reprinting in the "Petite Collection Maspero" of a work originally published in 1936.

[44] Reprinted in Nizan, *Intellectuel communiste*, pp. 246-51. Citation from p. 246.

[45] *Ibid*. One could argue that Nizan is still right on this question, but by the fourth quarter of the twentieth century, a new factor has been added. If culture as it is acquired by good, sensitive students, in all disciplines, from mechanical engineering to the classics, still has this corrosive effect, the emergent will to transform runs up against a rationally acquired blank wall. In other words, society appears to be so perfectly autoregulated, so powerfully reified, that it seems objectively impossible to change it even slightly. Hence the turn toward drugs and other forms of escape which are parasitical but not revolutionary is explicable in Nizan's terms, though he would find these phenomena depressing.

[46] *Correspondance André Gide—Roger Martin du Gard*, Vol. i, Jean Delay, ed. (Paris, 1968), p. 553. Letter of July 18, 1932.

[47] Cited in abbreviated form as the epigraph to this chapter. See note 1 above.

[48] See Chapter i, note 46, for further bibliography.

[49] Nizan, *Les Chiens de garde*, p. 13.

[50] *Ibid.*, p. 14.

[51] *Ibid.*, p. 15.

[52] *Ibid*. Those scholars who view Marxism as a rather simple determinist doctrine may find this remark surprising. Nizan goes on to draw a parallel with the current exploitation of workers, anarchy caused by the Depression, etc. These events are not in his view simple deviations from a "beatific destiny of humanity" (*ibid.*, pp. 15-16).

[53] *Ibid.*, p. 18.

[54] *Ibid.*, p. 22.

[55] *Ibid.*, p. 34.

[56] *Ibid.*, p. 23.

[57] *Ibid.*, p. 49.

[58] *Ibid.*, p. 24.

[59] Cited in Jack Newfield, *A Prophetic Minority* (New York, 1966), p. 20.

[60] Nizan, *Les Chiens de garde*, p. 26.

[61] Brunschvicg (1869-1944) was one of the favorite targets of Nizan's scorn. However, when Brunschvicg met Nizan and Sartre in the *NRF* offices in June 1939, he rather charitably congratulated

Sartre for having written *Les Chiens de garde*, "even though, you didn't spare me at all" (Sartre, "Avant-Propos," p. 19). In 1940 Brunschvicg was forced to flee Paris as a victim of Nazi anti-Semitism.

[62] Nizan, *Les Chiens de garde*, p. 28.

[63] *Ibid.*, p. 42.

[64] *Ibid.*

[65] *Ibid.*, p. 43.

[66] See Chapter VI, "The Dilemma of Political Involvement," in my *Roger Martin du Gard* (Ithaca, 1967).

[67] Nizan, *Les Chiens de garde*, p. 68.

[68] Cf. the passages from *Le Cheval de Troie* cited in Chapter I, notes 58 and 59. Also "Les Conséquences du refus," first published in the *NRF* in December 1932, and reprinted in Nizan, *Intellectuel communiste*, pp. 235-39, and *La Conspiration*, pp. 47 and *passim*. During the years 1924-1928, the group of young revolutionaries portrayed in Nizan's novel ". . . signed manifestoes which engaged them much less than their parents believed."

[69] Nizan, *Les Chiens de garde*, p. 68.

[70] Cf. Orwell's *The Road to Wigan Pier* (London, 1962), p. 140 (first published in 1937). Orwell scorns middle-class revolutionaries who are in truth frauds and have no real contact with the working class. Many of them who are "ardent Socialists" at 25, evolve into "sniffish Conservatives" by the age of 35. Perhaps, Orwell writes, "this class-breaking business isn't as simple as it looked! On the contrary, it is a wild ride in the darkness, and it may be that at the end of it the smile will be on the face of the tiger. With loving though slightly patronizing smiles we set out to greet our proletarian brothers—and behold! our proletarian brothers—in so far as we understand them—are not asking for our greetings, they are asking us to commit suicide."

[71] Nizan, *Les Chiens de garde*, p. 77.

[72] *Ibid.*, p. 105.

[73] Nizan finds Emile Durkheim's "moral propaganda" especially noxious (*Les Chiens de garde*, pp. 108-111).

[74] "Fascism and the Intellectuals," in S. J. Woolf, ed., *The Nature of Fascism* (New York, 1968), p. 209.

[75] Cf. Nizan, "Les Enfants de la lumière," in *Intellectuel communiste*, pp. 219-25, an article first published in *Commune*, No. 3, 1933. Nizan is here convinced that personalism would lead to fascism, the real revolutionary movement which the avant-garde Christians, "the children of light," are preparing. In actuality, Emmanuel Mounier never developed a sympathy for fascism, and after his brief flirtation with the Vichy régime, spent time in prison during the Oc-

cupation. There is, however, evidence of a personalist influence on the *Révolution Nationale* doctrine of the Vichy régime. See Robert Aron, *Histoire de Vichy* (Paris, 1954), pp. 271, 275, 279. Also see Chapter I, above, note 60.

[76] Nizan, *Les Chiens de garde*, p. 133.

[77] *Ibid.*, p. 137.

[78] *Ibid.*

[79] Lefebvre was one of the better minds attracted to communism in the 1930s. His denunciation of Nizan, and his partial retraction after his own turn came to leave the Party in 1958, are discussed in several sources. See especially, Ginsbourg, *Nizan*, pp. 87-88.

[80] *Ibid.*, p. 120.

[81] The Roger Garaudy case was given detailed coverage in the American and French press. See especially the articles in *Le Monde hebdomadaire* (January 1-7, 1970), p. 8; (February 5-11, 1970), p. 9; (May 21-27, 1970), p. 5.

[82] Sartre, "Avant-Propos," p. 58.

[83] The François Maspero reprint cites 1938 as the date of original publication by the *Editions Sociales Internationales*. This is an error. I am grateful to Professor Evalyn Clark for providing me with a copy of the first edition.

[84] Nizan, *Les Matérialistes de l'Antiquité*, p. 8.

[85] *Ibid.*, p. 14.

[86] *Ibid.*, pp. 16-17.

[87] *Ibid.*, p. 31.

[88] *Ibid.*, p. 33.

[89] *Ibid.*, p. 133. It is quite striking that Nizan makes no mention of revolution, or engagement, and speaks only of knowledge.

[90] Sartre, "Avant-Propos," pp. 58-60 and *passim*.

[91] Nizan, "Sur un certain front unique," in *Pour une Nouvelle Culture*, p. 52. My italics. This essay was first published in *Europe*, January 1933.

[92] Nizan, "Nous te tendons la main, Catholique . . ." (review of *Catholicisme et communisme*, by Robert Honnert), in *Pour une Nouvelle Culture*, p. 255. The review was originally published in *L'Humanité*, April 3, 1937, and the title phrase, "We extend our hand to you, Catholic," is taken from a speech by Maurice Thorez.

[93] In *Pour une Nouvelle Culture*, pp. 158-63 (first published in *Le Monde*, June 6, 1935). Citation from p. 163.

[94] Cited in Simone de Beauvoir, *La Force de l'âge* (Paris, 1960), p. 417.

[95] In the last few months of his life Nizan probably held both attitudes at different times. In theory the two positions are of course mutually exclusive.

96 Nizan, "Correspondance de Guerre," in *Intellectuel communiste*, p. 261.

97 *Ibid.*, p. 262.

98 *Ibid.*

99 *Ibid.*, p. 268. Letter of December 20, 1939.

100 Nizan, *Aden Arabie*, p. 168.

101 The possibility of illusion must be emphasized here, since there is no way of empirically proving that party membership ever permitted true engagement rather than *embrigadement*.

102 Cf. Caute, *Communism and the French Intellectuals*, and especially Carter Jefferson, "Communism and the French Intellectuals, 1919-1923," *Comparative Studies in Society and History*, Vol. II, No. 3 (June 1969), pp. 241-57. Jefferson challenges some of Caute's arguments and proves quite conclusively that the Party was extremely distrustful, even actively denigrated its intellectuals, much earlier than Caute thought. On the other hand, Jean-Pierre Bernard has shown that in specific cases, when the adhesion of an intellectual of national or international prominence was at stake, the Party could be remarkably supple and allow substantial deviations from official doctrine. The case in question is that of Henri Barbusse. See Bernard's excellent study, *Le Parti Communiste Français et la question littéraire* (Grenoble, 1972), esp. pp. 72-74.

103 The resurgence of engagement in the 1960s was of course outside the official communist parties and often in direct conflict with their stated policies. See especially Daniel and Gabriel Cohn-Bendit, *Obsolete Communism* (New York, 1969). One can never be certain, but it seems highly unlikely that full-fledged communist party membership will ever again become attractive to large groups of Western European intellectuals, unless the national communist parties break completely from Moscow and from ideological rigidity, thus becoming unrecognizable as communist parties. It is widely acknowledged that in Eastern Europe the official parties and the official party journals are spurned by many of the most creative intellectuals.

CHAPTER IV

1 ("I know all too well that politics are bloody"), "Le Monde pharisien," *NRF* (August 1934), p. 309.

2 January 18, 1945. ("You, the clerk who has betrayed . . ."), in Jacques Isorni, *Le Procès de Robert Brasillach*, 2nd ed. (Paris, 1956), p. 137.

3 Paraphrasing Jean Plumyène and Raymond Lasierra, as cited in note 9 below.

4 "Sympathy for the Devil: Ideological Conflict Among Literary Intellectuals in Liberated France," unpublished paper delivered at the

Third Annual Conference on Twentieth-Century Literature, Louisville, Kentucky, 1975. I am grateful to Mr. Hoberman for a copy of this paper.

[5] From Volume III of Orwell's selected essays, as cited in H. L. Wesseling, "Robert Brasillach and the Seductiveness of Fascism" (*Robert Brasillach en de verlokking van het fascisme*), *Tijdschrift voor Geschiedenis*, Vol. 88, No. 3 (1975), p. 1 (unpublished English translation by Aram Schimmer).

[6] Most of the important works available in English and French will be cited in this chapter. For a good bibliography up-to-date through 1959, see Paul Sérant, *Le Romantisme fasciste* (Paris, 1959), pp. 309-21. For a general bibliography, see the listings at the end of chapters in Hans Rogger and Eugen Weber, eds., *The European Right: A Historical Profile* (Berkeley, 1965).

[7] Many examples could be cited: The tremendous debate which erupted after the publication of Hannah Arendt's *Eichmann in Jerusalem* in 1963 had just about cooled when Albert Speer's *Inside the Third Reich* became a best seller in 1970. The cultural and political crisis in America in the 1960s elicited fears that we were in a situation similar to that of Germany in the early 1930s. The question of "Weimar Parallels" was reviewed in two thoughtful articles by Carl Schorske in the *New York Review of Books* (May 7 and 21, 1970). In 1976 Peter Gay reexamined "the German question, which has long haunted the civilized world," and found it "as acute as ever" ("Thinking about the Germans," *New York Times* [August 3, 1976], p. 29). As of this writing, another debate has begun, which promises to be bitter, over the publication of David Irving's semiapologetic treatment of the Fuehrer in *Hitler's War* (New York, 1977). For a balanced review of this and three other recent works on Hitler, see Alan Bullock, "The Schicklgruber Story," *New York Review of Books* (May 26, 1977), pp. 10-15.

[8] For a fascinating discussion of the propensity of liberal commentators to equate "the American youth revolt of the 1960s with the European youth revolt of the 1930s," thus tarring the former with the fascist brush, see Robert J. Soucy, "French Fascist Intellectuals in the 1930s: An Old New Left?," *French Historical Studies*, Vol. VIII, No. 3 (Spring 1974), pp. 445-58 (citation from p. 446).

[9] Jean Plumyène and Raymond Lasierra, *Les Fascismes français, 1923-1963* (Paris, 1963), p. 9.

[10] Robert Soucy, probably the most astute American-born student of the French Right, has pointed out that French conservatism and French fascism had more of a kinship than conservatives have wanted to admit. He demonstrates quite persuasively that the lines between the two movements were never "as distinct and tidy as has

been suggested, and furthermore, that the two philosophies shared many common denominators which were often far more important in determining their political behavior than the elements which separated them" (from "The Nature of Fascism in France," in Nathanael Greene, ed., *Fascism. An Anthology* [New York, 1968], p. 281).

[11] Plumyène and Lasierra, *Les Fascismes français*, p. 9. Their italics.

[12] *Ibid.*

[13] See Ernst Nolte, *Three Faces of Fascism*, Leila Vennewitz, tr. (New York, 1966), pp. 3-21.

[14] The one possible exception would be Maurice Bardèche, who caused somewhat of a stir in 1961 by publishing a reaffirmation of his commitment to fascism, *Qu'est-ce que le Fascisme?* Bardèche's title was calculated to be inflammatory, paraphrasing as it did the title of a famous work of an ideological enemy, Jean-Paul Sartre (*Qu'est-ce que la littérature?*, 1948). For a discussion of Bardèche, see Soucy, "The Nature of Fascism in France," pp. 275-76.

[15] Author of *Les Deux Etendards* and *Les Décombres*, who collaborated with Brasillach on *Je suis partout*, and was also sentenced to death but reprieved. After his release from prison in 1952 he wrote for extreme right newspapers. (See the obituary article in *Le Monde hebdomadaire*, August 31-September 6, 1972, p. 14.)

[16] George Steiner, "Preface," to J. S. McClelland, ed., *The French Right. From de Maistre to Maurras* (New York, 1970), p. 6.

[17] The case of Pound is a fascinating one but cannot be examined in detail here. In the past there had been a tendency among his admirers to play down his fascism. However, his commitment to fascism has been fully documented by C. David Heymann in *Ezra Pound: The Last Rower. A Political Profile* (New York, 1976). Heymann had access to the official records of Pound's work for Mussolini's regime, thanks to the Freedom of Information Act. The phrase "fascistic zeal" comes from Richard Ellman's review of Heymann's book in the *New York Times Book Review* (April 4, 1976), p. 25. Donald Davie, author of two biographies of Pound, finds flaws in Heymann's study, but still argues that "Pound was a fascist, profoundly, and no amount of talk about his affinities with Whitman will save him for democracy, nor will any attempt to treat his anti-Semitism as an unrelated pathological aberration" ("Pound and Fascism," *New York Review of Books*, April 1, 1976, p. 21).

[18] I am grateful to John M. Hoberman for this information. Hoberman has completed a dissertation on "The Psychology of the Collaborator in the Norwegian Novel," which when published will offer an important comparative perspective.

[19] H. L. Wesseling, "Robert Brasillach and the Seductiveness of Fascism," p. 4.

[20] *Ibid.* My italics.

[21] William R. Tucker, *The Fascist Ego. A Political Biography of Robert Brasillach* (Berkeley, 1975), p. ix. My italics.

[22] Cf. especially, *ibid.*, p. 17. Though he has no definitive proof, Tucker thinks that Brasillach's writings show that he "deliberately sought out a cause through which he might well make the ultimate sacrifice of the self." This would help to explain the martyr complex that appears from time to time in Brasillach's writings and is especially manifested in his great admiration for Joan of Arc, which dates at least from 1936 (see his *Animateurs du théâtre* [Paris, 1936], pp. 118-20). Tucker adds that "A basic character trait was his unshakable belief that he had been born into a world without hope of redemption through the Establishment." (The latter statement could of course also apply to a communist intellectual like Paul Nizan or a left Catholic like Emmanuel Mounier.) Tucker adopts the language of modern sociology, arguing that Brasillach "was never socialized." He was one of those "marginal men" described by Daniel Lerner et al. in *The Nazi Elite*. Tucker also offers some perceptive remarks about the quality of infantilism in Brasillach (pp. 21ff.), who like a child always "resisted discipline."

[23] Kurt H. Wolff, "For a Sociology of Evil," *Journal of Social Issues*, Vol. 25, No. 1 (1969), pp. 111-12.

[24] *Ibid.*, p. 113.

[25] Steiner, "Preface," p. 5.

[26] Beard's famous 1935 essay, "That Noble Dream," played a major role in discrediting the nineteenth-century Germanic historiographical tradition which had argued that "objective truth" could be discovered by the historian. Beard's essay is reprinted in Fritz Stern, ed., *The Varieties of History* (New York, 1956), pp. 315-28. Already in 1900 Croce believed in "the radical subjectivity of historical knowledge" (H. Stuart Hughes, *Consciousness and Society* [New York, 1958], p. 65).

[27] A useful model in this context is Eugen Weber's *Action Française* (Stanford, 1962). In researching this important study Weber was granted seventy interviews and had access to Charles Maurras's private papers. Most of those who helped Weber were conservatives who had been sympathetic to the *Action Française*. "They knew my interest in the Action Française did not mean agreement; they helped me in the belief that objective treatment would be better than either prejudice or panegyrics. I hope the results will bear them out. I doubt whether they will agree with my conclusions; for that matter, I doubt whether their enemies will. But I hope they will be able to recognize a determined effort to be fair" (Preface, p. x).

[28] Wolff, "For a Sociology of Evil," p. 115.

[29] In his autobiography, *Notre Avant-Guerre*, Brasillach wrote that February 6, 1934, marked "the exact date of social nationalism in our country" (Paris, 1941, p. 151).

[30] In addition to the volume prepared by Isorni, cited in note 2 above, it is discussed in all the biographies of Brasillach, and has been the subject of a full-length book, Charles Ambroise-Colin, *Un Procès de l'épuration: Robert Brasillach* (Paris, 1971).

[31] Page 212 of the Isorni transcript of the trial, page 50 of the "Livre de Poche" edition of the novel (Paris, 1973).

[32] Cited in Pol Vandromme, *Robert Brasillach. L'Homme et l'oeuvre* (Paris, 1956), p. 116.

[33] "Oeil pour oeil," *Les Temps modernes*, Vol. 1, No. 5 (February 1946), p. 823.

[34] (New York, 1968), p. 163. For example, the first case to come before the Paris *cour de justice* was that of Georges Suarez, "who had been lavishly paid by *Aujourd'hui* for promoting collaboration, affirming that informing on *résistants* was a sacred duty, and repeatedly calling for the stepping up of executions of Jews and Communists" (*ibid.*, p. 162).

[35] Whether or not we are persuaded of the validity of making this comparison, employing it was a good tactical move, given the profound sense of their national history which so many of the French possess. Chénier was executed just two days before Robespierre's fall and the end of the Reign of Terror. Like Brasillach, Chénier was young, only 31 at the time of his death.

[36] Both the defense and the prosecution lawyers lived on the same floor in the same apartment building, and the prosecutor had loyally served the previous regime, arguing cases in the same courtroom.

[37] This information from the special supplement of *Le Monde* dedicated to Brasillach (February 7, 1970), p. IV. Article by Agnès Fontaine, "Face à ses lecteurs d'aujourd'hui."

[38] A position of high prestige in France, which can lead to membership in the *Académie Française*. I know of no other example of someone so young being made responsible for the literary page of a major French newspaper.

[39] Pierre-Marie Dieudonnat, *Je suis partout 1930-1944. Les Maurrassiens devant la tentation fasciste* (Paris, 1973), p. 8. In his extreme and extremely diversified productivity, Brasillach resembles his fellow *normalien* Paul Nizan, who also died at age 35, but it will be recalled under very different circumstances.

[40] Isorni, *Le Procès de Brasillach*, p. 125.

[41] *Ibid.*, pp. 126-27.

[42] *Ibid.*, p. 127.

[43] It would serve no purpose to detail these citations here. They are scurrilous, vicious, scatological, and call openly for the summary execution of political enemies. An extensive sampling in English translation is available in William R. Tucker's book (esp. pp. 193-97, 231, and 271).

[44] *Ibid.*, p. 137.

[45] Reprinted in *ibid.*, p. 220.

[46] *Ibid.*, pp. 1-4. (Introduction to the 1956 edition of the trial transcript.)

[47] (Paris, 1964), p. 216.

[48] *Mémoires de guerre*, Vol. III, *Le Salut* (Paris, 1959), p. 127.

[49] *Ibid.*

[50] This curious linkage is noted by Wesseling, Tucker, and other Brasillach scholars. See Brasillach's novel *Les Sept Couleurs* (Paris, 1939, "Livre de Poche" edition, 1966), pp. 104-5 of paperback edition. All citations from *Les Sept Couleurs* will be from this edition. Brasillach also entitles the sixth chapter of his memoirs, *Notre Avant-Guerre*, "Ce mal du siècle, le fascisme. . . ." If Brasillach had remained faithful to the original intent of Alfred de Musset, when he described the *mal du siècle* in the famous first two chapters of *La Confession d'un enfant du siècle* (1835), fascism would have been portrayed as his *cure* for the *mal du siècle*.

[51] Though the theory of fascist romanticism is also supported by reputable scholars such as Raoul Girardet. See his important essay, "Notes sur l'Esprit d'un fascisme français," *Revue française de science politique*, Vol. 5, No. 3 (July-September, 1955), esp. p. 532, where he states that the spirit of fascism can be termed a romanticism, and p. 546.

[52] (Paris, 1959). For Brasillach, see especially p. 87, where Sérant speaks of "that romanticism of youth which led Brasillach to fascism."

[53] Vandromme, *Brasillach*, p. 110.

[54] *Ibid.*, p. 74. Vandromme also speaks of the February 6, 1934, riots as a moment "when pure and stoic youth were abandoned by impotent and cowardly leaders" (*ibid.*; the reference is to Charles Maurras, who would not step forward to lead a *coup d'état*).

[55] *Ibid.*, p. 81.

[56] *Ibid.*, p. 82. Brasillach's complex relationship with Maurras will be discussed briefly later in this chapter. For a fuller treatment, see Tucker, *The Fascist Ego*, Chap. III, "Maurras."

[57] Vandromme, *Brasillach*, p. 110.

[58] *Ibid.*, p. 220. Other references to Brasillach's romanticism may be found on pp. 66, 70-71, 76, 78, 80, and 87.

[59] René Rémond, in his classic study of the French Right, gives a membership figure of 250,000 for the *PPF* in 1937 (*La Droite en France* [Paris, 1954], p. 217).

[60] Frédéric J. Grover, *Drieu la Rochelle and the Fiction of Testimony* (Berkeley, 1958), p. 51.

[61] In addition to the Grover biography cited in the previous note and several important articles by Robert Soucy, Frank Field puts Drieu in an interesting perspective in his *Three French Writers and the Great War. Studies in the Rise of Communism and Fascism* (New York, 1975).

[62] "Romanticism and Realism in the Fascism of Drieu la Rochelle," *Journal of the History of Ideas*, Vol. 31, No. 1 (January-March 1970), pp. 74-75.

[63] Suicide is also a major theme in *L'Homme à cheval*, and two major characters in *Gilles* take their own lives, while the hero meditates frequently on the subject of suicide. At the end of the novel the hero voluntarily chooses to die while defending Franquist lines against a republican attack in the Spanish Civil War.

[64] Soucy, "Romanticism and Realism," p. 69.

[65] "Unité Française et Unité Allemande," *Europe*, No. 133 (January 15, 1934), p. 34.

[66] Soucy, "Romanticism and Realism," p. 76.

[67] Printed in *Les Cahiers de "Bravo"* (Paris, August 1931). Citation from p. 11.

[68] Pierre Drieu la Rochelle, *Gilles* (Paris, 1939; citation from "Livre de Poche" edition, Paris, 1968), p. 352. See also *ibid.*, p. 347.

[69] Soucy, "Romanticism and Realism," p. 83.

[70] *Ibid.*, p. 90.

[71] "Fascism and the Intellectuals," in S. J. Woolf, ed., *The Nature of Fascism* (New York, 1968), pp. 214-15. My italics.

[72] For Benda's attack on realist *clercs*, see especially above, Chapter II.

[73] Field, *Three French Writers and the Great War*, esp. pp. 81-135.

[74] *Portraits* (Paris, 1935), p. 237.

[75] *Ibid.*, p. 238. My italics.

[76] Tucker, *The Fascist Ego*, p. 271 (quoting a *Je suis partout* article by Brasillach dated October 23, 1942).

[77] The cadets reincarnate the soul of Spain, whereas the republicans are "Marxist gangs who were terrorizing the entire country." Though Brasillach was not a practicing Catholic, Catholic propaganda was used in this pamphlet; the cadets put up a shrine in honor of the Immaculate Conception and during their defense "The Blessed Virgin was smiling upon them." "This is the gospel of the

new Knights of the Alcazar. From them the world is learning anew the eternal truth." The brochure concludes as follows: "Twice, against Moors and Turks, at Granada and at Lepanto, Spain delivered Western civilization from the Oriental peril. It is against another peril that Spain is standing up again, against a subtler Orient and one which is perhaps more tyrannical. In the crusade against Bolshevism, Spain claims the honor of the first danger and the first victory" (citations from the English edition, tr. anon. [New York: Fordham University Alumnae (*sic*) Association, 1937], pp. 25, 28, and 56).

[78] *Histoire de la guerre d'Espagne* (Paris, 1939), p. 36. Cf. p. 106, where they do admit the courage of the republican forces and regret that Franco was not able to take Madrid immediately in 1936. Still, when the first battles were over the nationalists held a good portion of Spain, "because of a profound defense reaction of the entire nation, and this communion between the Spanish people and the insurgent troops, . . . The quick coup failed, but it served as a signal for the war of liberation."

[79] *Ibid.*, p. 438.

[80] Brasillach, *Animateurs du théâtre*, p. 146.

[81] *Ibid.*, pp. 217-18.

[82] *Ibid.*, p. 48.

[83] This is true in all his novels, even the openly propagandistic *Les Sept Couleurs* (published in 1939, when Brasillach turned 30). See pp. 141-60, the extended discussion of what it means to turn 30, and the consequent *angoisse du vieillissement* (anguish of aging).

[84] Robert Brasillach, *Comme le Temps passe* (Paris, 1937, "Livre de Poche" edition, Paris, 1963), citation from paperback edition, p. 194.

[85] *Ibid.*, p. 433.

[86] Robert Brasillach, *L'Enfant de la nuit* (Paris, 1934), p. 254.

[87] The action takes place in November 1943, and at that late date the Germans are such gentle occupiers that if someone is caught on the streets after the curfew all he has to do is shine boots in headquarters until 5 A.M. (*Six Heures à perdre*, Paris, 1953, p. 42). The members of the Resistance are portrayed as far worse than the Germans, as bandits and terrorists (p. 37), who go around murdering innocent citizens who were "without political activity" (p. 206).

[88] Vandromme, *Brasillach*, pp. 59, 89, 185, 190-91, Sérant, *Le Romantisme fasciste*, pp. 86-90 and *passim*.

[89] Tucker, *The Fascist Ego*, pp. 27ff. Tucker would go as far as to label Brasillach an "anarchofascist" (p. 27) or "right wing anarchist" (p. 29). Tucker returns to the question of anarchism in Brasillach

later, noting the unresolved paradox because there was in Brasillach "a penchant for anarchism and a desire for the reintegration of isolated individuals into a national community . . ." (p. 146).

[90] Brasillach, *Notre Avant-Guerre*, p. 31.

[91] See Tucker, *The Fascist Ego*, p. 125. In his gang, Brasillach found a special brand of comradeship, with "overtones of juvenile delinquency" and "adolescent roguishness."

[92] Brasillach, *Notre Avant-Guerre*, pp. 35, 37.

[93] Vandromme, *Brasillach*, p. 164.

[94] See p. 121n19.

[95] See David Caute, *Communism and the French Intellectuals* (New York, 1964), pp. 96-99 and 154.

[96] Brasillach, *Notre Avant-Guerre*, pp. 219, 312.

[97] His essays have been collected and published by Gallimard under the title *Descriptions critiques*.

[98] This information came to light during the dispute over whether or not the critic and editor Jean Paulhan had signed the petition. Lawyer Isorni produced the document, and the page which had Paulhan's signature on it also included Roy's, crossed out (*Le Monde*, supplement to No. 7810, February 21, 1970, "Correspondance," p. v). Reading about this incident brought forth a powerful sense of *déjà vu*, recalling the anguished doubts many intellectuals in America felt about whether or not to sign anti-Vietnam War petitions, when to be sure much less was at stake for them personally.

[99] Caute, *Communism and the French Intellectuals*, p. 154.

[100] Brasillach, *Notre Avant-Guerre*, pp. 27-28. My italics.

[101] *Ibid.*, pp. 205-6.

[102] Alastair Hamilton, *The Appeal of Fascism* (New York, 1971), p. 212.

[103] See Weber, *Action Française*, p. 452. It could be argued that Brasillach finally became a true romantic when he broke with Maurras who had always detested romanticism and had prided himself on his realism. Pol Vandromme, despite his usual emphasis on Brasillach's romanticism, gives a somewhat different interpretation. Vandromme refers to the extremely critical essay Brasillach wrote on Drieu la Rochelle in 1934 (cited above, note 75). At that time Brasillach practically worshiped Maurras. By 1943, after the break with the founder of the *Action Française*, Brasillach had become much more indulgent, even favorably inclined toward Drieu la Rochelle, praising the lucidity of his articles. Vandromme suggests that under the pressure of historical events Brasillach came to ally himself more and more with the younger fascists, "the buddies of the group" (*les*

copains du groupe), and that he came to prefer "comrades over mentors" (Vandromme, *Brasillach*, p. 216).

[104] Brasillach, *Notre Avant-Guerre*, p. 168.

[105] *Ibid.*, p. 271.

[106] *Ibid.*, p. 283.

[107] Brasillach, *Les Sept Couleurs*, p. 158. My italics.

[108] *Ibid.*, p. 106. (Brasillach experimented with seven different literary modes in this novel; this particular section is in the form of a journal kept by one of the two heroes of the novel who is living in Germany and observing the fascist scene.)

[109] Brasillach's anticommunism is undisputed and indisputable. Citations to this effect can be multiplied. One of the most striking is the pro-Franco passage cited in note 76 above, where Brasillach and his co-author Henri Massis elaborate on the theme of bolshevism as an Oriental despotism. Cf. also Brasillach's letter to Lucien Rebatet of August 1943: "I am against bolshevism because it is total death" (cited in Dieudonnat, *Je suis partout 1930-1944*, p. 366). On the other hand, the genuineness of his antibourgeois sentiments is open to question. It is undeniable that his first two novels (*Le Voleur d'étincelles*, 1932, and *L'Enfant de la nuit*, 1934) extol traditional bourgeois values of thrift, order, property, and family loyalty.

[110] William R. Tucker, "Politics and Aesthetics: The Fascism of Robert Brasillach," *Western Political Quarterly*, Vol. xv, No. 4 (December 1962), p. 616.

[111] Isorni, *Le Procès de Robert Brasillach*, pp. 143-45, 148-49, and especially p. 150, where the prosecutor calls Brasillach's resignation from *Je suis partout* in September 1943 a "simple maneuver of opportunism."

[112] Tucker notes that Brasillach exposed himself to the "justifiable suspicion that he used the collaboration movement as a vehicle for keeping his name before the public." Writers know that a period of enforced silence can damage a literary reputation, and no one could be certain how long the period of German domination would last. "If Germany turned out to be the agent of the *Weltgeist* and established the New Order as the next historical epoch, might not those intellectuals who wrote only noncommittal books be under a cloud of suspicion because of their timidity? Would not those who resorted to the underground press lose their very identity as persons as well as intellectuals?" Tucker concludes that some took these risks, but Brasillach desired to be in the public eye, and accepted rightist patronage from the outset of his career (*The Fascist Ego*, p. 276).

[113] Cf. George Orwell's prediction made in 1937 that when the "pinch" came, when fascist domination of the European continent

became more than a frightening possibility, the "main movement of the intelligentsia [would] be toward Fascism" (*The Road to Wigan Pier* [London, 1962, first published 1937], p. 185).

[114] *Humanisme et terreur* (Paris, 1947), pp. 41-47.

[115] The book is subtitled "Essay on the Communist Problem." It was first published as a series of essays in *Les Temps modernes*, and they "raised a storm of protest from the political right as well as some disagreement from the political left" (Albert Rabil, Jr., *Merleau-Ponty* [New York, 1967], p. 102).

[116] Cited in Dieudonnat, *Je suis partout 1930-1944*, p. 366.

[117] Tucker, *The Fascist Ego*, p. 232.

[118] A pun. *Je suis parti*—I have left—refers to the collaborators who were escorted across the frontier by the retreating Nazis to the baroque castle of Sigmaringen, where a shadow government in exile was set up. This whole episode was savagely satirized by Louis-Ferdinand Céline in *D'un Château l'autre* (Paris, 1957).

[119] *Ibid.*, pp. 276-77.

[120] *Les Fascismes français*, p. 186.

[121] Novick, *The Resistance versus Vichy*, pp. 187-88.

[122] Drieu committed suicide; Céline spent time in prison but was released and died in 1962; on Rebatet see note 15 above. A. de Châteaubriant went to Germany in April 1944, remained there after the war. He was condemned to death in absentia in November 1948, but in the interim had returned to religious orthodoxy and was never repatriated. He died in the Tyrol in 1951. Abel Bonnard went with Pétain to Sigmaringen and thence to Spain where he remained. He was condemned to death in absentia and in 1958 returned to France to defend himself. He was not executed. (This information from Sérant, *Le Romantisme fasciste*, Chap. x.)

[123] Originally published in *L'Express*, November 28, 1957, and reprinted in the special supplement of *Le Monde* dedicated to Brasillach (February 7, 1970), p. iv.

[124] Agnès Fontaine, "Face à ses lecteurs d'aujourd'hui," *Le Monde* (February 7, 1970), p. iv.

[125] *The Journal of Psychohistory*, Vol. 4, No. 1 (Summer 1976), pp. 71-92.

[126] These themes are present in all his works, going back at least to *The Man Covered with Women* (*L'Homme couvert de femmes*), published in 1925, and *Le Jeune Européen* (1927). The latter work is primarily concerned with a perceived crisis of civilization, but includes such incidental remarks as "Men are born only for war, as women are made only in order to produce children" (p. 15).

[127] Soucy, "Psycho-Sexual Aspects of the Fascism of Drieu la Rochelle," p. 83.

[128] René Etiemble, in *Littérature dégagée, 1942-1953* (Paris, 1955), p. 168, states openly that Brasillach was a homosexual. Maurice Martin du Gard in his *Chronique de Vichy* described Brasillach as "dreamy and effeminate" (cited in Hamilton, *The Appeal of Fascism*, p. 245).

[129] Tucker, *The Fascist Ego*, p. 276. See *ibid.*, p. 290, where Tucker reviews the whole question, noting that he has evidence that at one point in his life Brasillach had a mistress. Also pp. 127-28, where Tucker observes that psychological factors were surely at work in Brasillach's "exaltation of the physically fit, animallike young fascists," since he was short, wore horn-rimmed glasses, had small hands and a tendency toward corpulence. He was the "prototype of the cultivated intellectual." "Envy was present, perhaps—or Eros."

[130] The near-worship of masculinity is especially prevalent in *Le Feu follet*, *Gilles*, and *L'Homme à cheval*. See Soucy, "Psycho-Sexual Aspects of the Fascism of Drieu la Rochelle," esp. pp. 72-74 and 87-88. Soucy makes an unassailable case for the presence of a strong sadistic element in Drieu's treatment of women, citing a passage describing brutal torture of a woman and one where Drieu fantasizes that he is cutting off a prostitute's head.

[131] As a case in point, there is the interview with the retired British intelligence officer in *The Sorrow and the Pity* (1971), Marcel Ophuls's great documentary film on the Occupation and the Resistance. The man, who was parachuted behind enemy lines, was an admitted homosexual.

[132] "The Unsuccessful Adolescence of Heinrich Himmler," *American Historical Review*, Vol. 76, No. 3 (June 1971), pp. 612-41, and "The Psychohistorical Origins of the Nazi Youth Cohort," *American Historical Review*, Vol. 76, No. 5 (December 1971), pp. 1457-1502.

[133] Hamilton, *The Appeal of Fascism*, p. 18.

[134] "Introduction," to the Mentor Classics Edition of Machiavelli, *The Prince* (New York, 1952), p. 22.

[135] An interesting review of this debate is given in John Hoberman's unpublished paper, "Sympathy for the Devil," cited in note 4 above.

[136] He called for burning the republican leader Sarraut and wrote in *Je suis partout*, October 24, 1936, that ". . . when Mm. Cot and Blum have been shot in good and proper legal form by a national government, no tears will be shed over these excrements, but champagne will be drunk by French families" (as cited in Tucker, *The Fascist Ego*, p. 197). Prosecutor Reboul cited Brasillach's remark about Jewish children to telling effect during his trial.

[137] *Les Sept Couleurs*, p. 157. Cf. Robert Soucy's fascinating dis-

cussion of Philippe Barrès, son of the protofascist intellectual Maurice Barrès. Philippe had been very sympathetic to Nazism, but when France fell in 1940 joined General de Gaulle in London. Soucy suggests that Brasillach's contrasting behavior may be explained as a conflict in priorities. "Although both thinkers in the 1930s had strongly admired the 'national revival' they had witnessed in Hitler Germany, Brasillach ultimately placed a higher value on the *homo fascista* than on territorial sovereignty" (*Fascism in France. The Case of Maurice Barrès* [Berkeley, 1972], p. 314).

[138] The presence of Camus's name on this list is especially interesting to the intellectual historian. As late as January 11, 1945, Camus had been arguing in the pages of *Combat* for severe and swift punishment for collaborators (cited in Plumyène and Lasierra, *Les Fascismes français*, p. 186). Camus made an effort "to steel himself intellectually against his own feelings on the subject of capital punishment" (Emmet Parker, *Albert Camus: The Artist in the Arena* [Madison, 1965], p. 83). The question of whether or not it had been just to demand the lives of guilty collaborators was to become a "major issue" for Camus, and was "eventually to affect the whole course of his political thought" (*ibid.*, pp. 84-86). As early as November 1944, he had doubts about the death penalty, but only with the Brasillach case did he actually change his mind. The effect of this new position can clearly be seen in the writing of *L'Homme revolté* (*The Rebel*), published in 1951. This work is a document of intellectual history of major significance, both in its own right and because it marks Camus' famous break with Jean-Paul Sartre. For a perceptive account of this quarrel, see Pierre-Henri Simon, *L'Esprit et l'histoire* (Paris, 1954), pp. 193-208. Also Germaine Brée, *Camus and Sartre. Crisis and Commitment* (New York, 1972).

[139] Benda's vehement attack on the "right to error" was briefly discussed in Chapter II above. For further details see his *Les Cahiers d'un clerc* (Paris, 1950), pp. 139-42, 178-81, 205-9.

[140] This question has painful and poignant overtones for an American who has lived through the period of America's involvement in Vietnam. Can we say in 1978 that our moral (and perhaps juridical) responsibilities regarding Vietnam have ceased? Because of the North Vietnamese victory in 1975 is the responsibility of the many distinguished intellectuals who assisted three presidents in planning and carrying out that war terminated? Or could these men someday be called out of retirement or away from the universities where they now teach and brought before some bar of justice? How far does the responsibility of intellectuals go? Perhaps only Noam Chomsky has faced this question with consistent lucidity.

[141] In Jacques Debû-Bridel, ed., *La Résistance intellectuelle* (Paris, 1970), pp. 93-94.

[142] Resulting not from activities during the Occupation, but because he published a defense of fascism, *Nüremberg ou la terre promise*, in 1948. The book was seized by the authorities and Bardèche went to jail (Plumyène and Lasierra, *Les Fascismes français*, p. 209).

[143] Etiemble, *Littérature dégagée*, p. 163.

[144] *Ibid.*, pp. 167-68.

[145] For an early and thoughtful review of this question which specifically comments on Chomsky's position, see Tom Wicker, "The Malaise Beyond Dissent," *New York Times* (March 12, 1967), p. E13.

[146] Herbert R. Southworth, *Le Mythe de la croisade de Franco* (Paris, 1964), p. 227.

[147] "Apologie pour un meurtre," *Le Monde* (February 6, 1975), p. 10. His comments on the "right to error" are especially pointed. Does the intellectual, he asks, belong to that "lordly race" (*race de seigneurs*), who flatter themselves in thinking that they have a great influence on history, but are scandalized if they are asked to pay the consequences for that influence, when those consequences are "of lead." In the upheaval among both camps of the intelligentsia concerning the Brasillach case, he perceives a common origin, an obscure fear of losing "these privileges, this pretentious immunity, this irresponsibility (for) our actions" (*irresponsabilité agissante*).

[148] *Ibid.*

[149] Published in three subsequent issues of *Le Monde*, including a letter from one of Brasillach's sisters, and an ironically entitled counter-attack by Pierre de Boisdeffre, *Apologie pour un condamné*.

[150] One may join Prosecutor Reboul, General de Gaulle, and Julien Benda in accusing Robert Brasillach of *trahison*. We may deny him the role of "bearer of consciousness," as much as he coveted it. But in Jan Myrdal's terms he was too fully engaged ever to be a "whore of reason."

CHAPTER V

[1] Francis Golffing, tr., *The Genealogy of Morals* (New York, 1956), p. 235.

[2] Especially in Chap. II, "Doing as One Likes," and the conclusions.

[3] For an early denunciation of intellectuals for their hidden political ambitions, see Georges Sorel, "Lettre à Daniel Halévy," in *Réflexions sur la violence*, 3rd ed. (Paris, 1912), pp. 51-52.

[4] Cf. Maurice Barrès' categorization of the Dreyfusist intellectuals as "platform anarchists" in *Scènes et doctrines du nationalisme* (Paris, 1902), p. 208.

[5] The example of the "Dump Johnson" movement is discussed in Chapter II. A striking illustration in the French context is found in a

speech by Robert Lacoste, the Resident Minister appointed to Algeria in 1956, who advocated and utilized extreme measures in order to suppress the Algerian independence movement. Speaking to a meeting of French veterans' organizations in July 1957, Lacoste stated: "The exhibitionists of the heart and the intellect who have mounted the campaign against the tortures *are responsible* for the re-surgence of terrorism, which has caused in Algiers in recent days twenty dead and one hundred-fifty wounded. I present them to you for your scorn" (*Je les voue à votre mépris*). Published in *Le Monde*, July 9, 1957, p. 4. My italics.

⁶ *Le Monde hebdomadaire* (November 13-19, 1969), p. 7.

⁷ In addition to the works cited and discussed previously, see Irv-ing Howe, "The New York Intellectuals," *Commentary*, Vol. 46, No. 4 (October 1968), pp. 29-51. For an intellectual's attack on his peers, see Thomas Molnar, *The Decline of the Intellectual* (New York, 1961), in which intellectuals are accused of utopianism, dogmatism, immorality, misconceptions about human nature, and other vices.

⁸ Talcott Parsons, " 'The Intellectual': A Social Role Category," in Philip Rieff, ed., *On Intellectuals* (New York, 1969), pp. 3-26. Edward Shils, "The Intellectuals and the Powers: Some Perspectives for Comparative Analysis," in *ibid.*, pp. 27-56.

⁹ J. P. Nettl, "Ideas, Intellectuals, and Structures of Dissent," in Rieff, ed., *On Intellectuals*, p. 66.

¹⁰ *Ibid.*, p. 83. Nettl's essay is a substantial piece of work, the longest in the Rieff collection, *On Intellectuals*. Nevertheless, it is by no means a complete treatment, and perhaps Nettl would have ex-panded it into a book had he lived. Surely he would have felt obliged to deal with what appears to be another category of thought, in addi-tion to the two he treats in his essay—namely the whole realm of aesthetic or literary thought, which is usually not *engagé*, and yet not academic.

¹¹ *Ibid.*, p. 88.

¹² *Ibid.* His italics. On several occasions Nettl qualifies his argu-ment by stressing that he is constructing an ideal type. No single in-dividual would think totally in terms of ideas of scope or of quality.

¹³ *Ibid.*, p. 81.

¹⁴ *Ibid.*, p. 90.

¹⁵ *Ibid.*, p. 97. From my observation at least, something like a nat-ural antipathy between two types of individuals seemed to surface again and again during the late 1960s whenever college professors gathered in groups.

¹⁶ *Ibid.*, p. 126.

¹⁷ *Ibid.*, p. 112. While, Nettl adds with some bitterness, prag-matists like Raymond Aron gloat happily at this impotence.

[18] *Ibid.*, p. 124.
[19] *Ibid.*, p. 129.
[20] *Ibid.*, p. 112.
[21] *Ibid.*, pp. 94-95.
[22] *Ibid.*, p. 131.
[23] *Ibid.*, p. 94.

[24] Or their pupils, those who aspire to become intellectuals. For an interesting discussion, which agrees with Nettl that the social role of the older type of intellectual is weakening, but which argues that the mantle of critical thought may pass on to a new group, a segment of the technocratic class, see Frédéric Bon and Michel-Antoine Burnier, *Les Nouveaux Intellectuels* (Paris, 1966), pp. 175-76 and *passim*. There is some evidence that this transition has begun to occur, but extensive new research must be done before any firm conclusions can be drawn. For a fascinating study of one incident of engagement which drew in scientists and engineers, see Dorothy Nelkin, *The University and Military Research* (Ithaca, 1972). Nelkin studies the effort (which eventually failed) to force M. I. T. to divest itself of the Instrumentation Laboratory, where a great deal of classified military research was conducted.

EPILOGUE

[1] Bernard Pingaud, "Introduction," in *Arc*, No. 30 (1966), "Sartre aujourd'hui," p. 1.

[2] See Chapter III for details of the new studies and translations of Nizan which have appeared since *Aden Arabie* was reprinted in 1960. As for Emmanuel Mounier, *Esprit* remains one of the most vigorous and independent periodicals published in France. Its evolution has been traced by Michel Winock in his *Histoire politique de la revue "Esprit" 1930-1950* (Paris, 1975). See also, Joseph A. Amato, *Mounier and Maritain: A French Catholic Understanding of the Modern World* (University, Ala., 1975), and R. William Rauch, Jr., *Politics and Belief in Contemporary France. Emmanuel Mounier and Christian Democracy, 1932-1950* (The Hague, 1972). Catholic engagement dramatically increased throughout the world during the 1960s, from Latin America to Sicily and Spain, from the USA to France, and has not subsided as rapidly in the 1970s as have other forms of engagement. Father Daniel Berrigan, the most famous *engagé* priest during the period of Vietnam protest in this country, spent several years studying in France, when the worker-priest movement was at its height. Berrigan was deeply influenced by the worker-priest movement and by Emmanuel Mounier, calling himself in his correspondence from France a "personalist." This is a remarkable example of the direct influence of one of the founders of the French doc-

trine of engagement on American engaged thought and action in the 1960s. (I am grateful to Anne Klejment of the State University of New York at Binghamton for this information.)

[3] *The Writings of Sartre*, 2 vols. (Evanston, 1975).

[4] Perhaps the best short biographical study is by his friend Francis Jeanson, *Sartre dans sa vie* (Paris, 1974).

[5] See especially, Michel-Antoine Burnier, *Les Existentialistes et la politique* (Paris, 1969). English translation, New York, 1969.

[6] Dominique Desanti, review of *Les Ecrits de Sartre*, by Michel Contat and Michel Rybalka, in *Le Monde hebdomadaire* (April 9-15, 1970), p. 13.

[7] On Desanti's past as a militant, see David Caute, *Communism and the French Intellectuals* (New York, 1964), pp. 177, 185, 229.

[8] On Sartre's arrest, see the unsigned article, "Un 'engagement' gauchiste," *Le Monde hebdomadaire* (June 17-23, 1971), p. 8.

[9] "What's Jean-Paul Sartre Thinking Lately?," *Esquire* (December 1972), pp. 206-7 (an interview with Pierre Bénichou, tr. Patricia Southgate).

[10] See "Sartre Accuses the Intellectuals of Bad Faith," *New York Times Magazine* (October 17, 1971), pp. 38ff. (an interview with John Gerassi, also printed in the *Manchester Guardian*, September 11, 1971). By June 1972, Sartre had come to believe that "engagement [in the sense of what he called 'meetings and signatures on manifestoes'] was no longer enough. I adopted another attitude. . . . Actually I am now all for illegal action" ("What's Jean-Paul Sartre Thinking Lately?," p. 207). See also Philippe Gavi, Jean-Paul Sartre, and Pierre Victor, *On a raison de se révolter* (Paris, 1974). This is a fascinating series of taped discussions, spanning a period of eighteen months, between Sartre and two young leftist militants. Though they are less than half his age, Sartre treats them as equals, sometimes even mentors.

[11] Published in three consecutive issues of *Le Nouvel Observateur* (June 23-July 7, 1975), and translated in an abridged version in the *New York Review of Books* (August 7, 1975), pp. 10-17.

[12] See Mark Poster, *Existential Marxism in Postwar France: From Sartre to Althusser* (Princeton, 1975).

[13] These oscillations have been widely discussed by biographers and by more or less scholarly polemicists. See especially, Caute, *Communism and the French Intellectuals*, pp. 247-58, and *passim*; Burnier, *Choice of Action*; and H. Stuart Hughes, *The Obstructed Path* (New York, 1968), pp. 170-226.

[14] "M. Jean-Paul Sartre et la violence," *Le Monde hebdomadaire* (April 30-May 6, 1970), p. 6. Sartre is doubtful that he will have

much posthumous influence. "He knows all too well that the role intellectuals play in the world is declining. He predicts, indeed hopes, that they will disappear inasmuch as they are 'men who think in the place of others' " (Bertrand Poirot-Delpech, citing Sartre in a review of *Situations* x [*Le Monde hebdomadaire*, January 22-28, 1976], p. 14).

Selected Bibliography

◊◊◊◊◊◊◊◊◊

BOOKS

Aaron, Daniel. *Writers on the Left*. New York: Avon, 1961.

Adereth, Maxwell. *Commitment in Modern French Literature. A Brief Study of 'Littérature Engagée' in the Works of Péguy, Aragon, and Sartre*. London: Victor Gollanz, 1967.

Ambroise-Colin, Charles. *Un Procès de l'épuration: Robert Brasillach*. Paris: Mame, 1971.

Arnold, Matthew. *Culture and Anarchy*. New York: Macmillan, 1925 (first published 1869).

Aron, Raymond. *The Opium of the Intellectuals*. Terence Kilmartin, tr. New York: Norton, 1962.

Aron, Robert. *Histoire de Vichy*. Paris: Fayard, 1954.

Barrès, Maurice. *Scènes et doctrines du nationalisme*. Paris: Plon, 1902.

de Beauvoir, Simone. *La Force de l'âge*. Paris: Gallimard, 1960.

―――. *Mémoires d'une jeune fille rangée*. Paris: Gallimard, 1958.

Benda, Julien. *Les Cahiers d'un clerc, 1936-1949*. Paris: Emile-Paul, 1950.

―――. *La Jeunesse d'un clerc*. Paris: Gallimard, 1936.

―――. *Précision, 1930-1937*. Paris: Gallimard, 1937.

―――. *La Trahison des clercs*. Paris: Grasset, 1958 (3rd ed., preface by René Etiemble; the 1975 edition, also published by Grasset, includes a new introduction by André Lwoff).

Berl, Emmanuel. *La Politique et les Partis*. Paris: Rieder, 1932.

Bernanos, Georges. *Les Grands Cimetières sous la lune*. Paris: Plon, 1938.

Bernard, Jean-Pierre A. *Le Parti Communiste Français et la question littéraire*. Grenoble: Presses Universitaires de Grenoble, 1972.

Bodin, Louis. *Les Intellectuels*. Paris: Presses Universitaires de France, 1964.

———, and Jean Touchard. *Front Populaire 1936*. Paris: Armand Colin, 1961.

Bon, Frédéric, and Michel-Antoine Burnier. *Les Nouveaux Intellectuels*. Paris: Editions Cujas, 1966.

Bourgin, Hubert. *De Jaurès à Léon Blum. L'Ecole Normale et la Politique*. Paris: Arthème Fayard, 1938.

Brachfeld, George I. *André Gide and the Communist Temptation*. Geneva: Droz, 1959.

Brasillach, Robert. *Animateurs du theatre*. Paris: Correa, 1936.

———. *Comme le Temps passe*. Paris: Plon, 1937.

———. *L'Enfant de la nuit*. Paris: La Palatine, 1934.

———. *Notre Avant-Guerre*. Paris: Plon, 1941.

———. *Portraits*. Paris: Plon, 1935.

———. *Les Quatres Jeudis*. Paris: Les Sept Couleurs, 1951.

———. *Les Sept Couleurs*. Paris, Plon, 1939.

———. *Six Heures à perdre*. Paris: Plon, 1953.

———. *Le Voleur d'étincelles*. Paris: Plon, 1935.

———, and Maurice Bardèche. *Histoire de la guerre d'Espagne*. Paris: Plon, 1939.

———, and Henri Massis. *The Cadets of the Alcazar*. Tr. annon. New York: Fordham University Alumnae (*sic*) Association, 1937.

Brée, Germaine, ed. *Camus. A Collection of Critical Essays*. Englewood Cliffs: Prentice-Hall, 1962.

———. *Camus and Sartre: Crisis and Commitment*. New York: Dell, 1972.

Bréhier, Emile, and Paul Ricoeur. *Histoire de la philosophie allemande*, 3rd ed. Paris: J. Vrin, 1954.

Brombert, Victor. *The Intellectual Hero. Studies in the French Novel 1880-1955*. Philadelphia: Lippincott, 1960.

Burnier, Michel-Antoine. *Les Existentialistes et la politique*. Paris: Gallimard, 1966. Translated as *Choice of Action*. New York: Random House, 1969.

Cassels, Alan. *Fascist Italy*. New York: Crowell, 1968.

Caudwell, Christopher. *Studies and Further Studies in a Dying Culture*. New York: Monthly Review Press, 1971.

Caute, David. *Communism and the French Intellectuals*. New York: Macmillan, 1964.

Céline, Louis-Ferdinand. *Mort à crédit*. Paris: Gallimard, 1952 (first published 1936).

————. *Voyage au bout de la nuit*. Paris: Gallimard, 1952 (first published 1932).

Claudel, Paul. *Poésie, Oeuvres complètes*, ii. Paris: Gallimard, 1952.

Cohn-Bandit, Daniel and Gabriel. *Obsolete Communism: The Left-Wing Alternative*. New York: McGraw-Hill, 1969.

Crossman, Richard, ed. *The God that Failed*. New York: Bantam Books, 1965 (first published 1950).

Debû-Bridel, Jacques, ed. *La Résistance intellectuelle*. Paris: Julliard, 1970.

Dieudonnat, Pierre-Marie. *Je suis partout, 1930-1944. Les Maurrassians devant la tentation fasciste*. Paris: La Table Ronde, 1973.

Drabovitch, W. *Les Intellectuels français et le Bolshévisme*. Paris: Les Libertés Françaises, 1938.

Drieu la Rochelle, Pierre. *La Comédie de Charleroi*. Paris: Gallimard, 1934.

————. *L'Eau frâiche*, play in 3 acts, printed in *Les Cahiers de "Bravo."* Paris: August 1931.

————. *Le Feu follet*. Paris: Gallimard, 1963 (first published 1931).

————. *Gilles*. Paris: Gallimard, 1968 (first published 1939).

————. *L'Homme à cheval*. Paris: Gallimard, 1943.

————. *Le Jeune Européen*. Paris: Gallimard, 1926.

Etiemble, René. *Littérature dégagée, 1942-1953*. Paris: Gallimard, 1955 (Vol. ii of *Hygiène des Lettres*).

Field, Frank. *Three French Writers and the Great War: Studies in the Rise of Communism and Fascism*. New York: Cambridge University Press, 1975.

Fleming, Donald, and Bernard Bailyn, eds. *The Intellectual

Migration. Cambridge: Harvard University Press, 1969.

Frings, Manfred G. *Max Scheler*. Pittsburgh: Duquesne University Press, 1965.

de Gaulle, Charles. *Mémoires de Guerre*, Vol. iii, *Le Salut*. Paris: Plon, 1959.

Gavi, Philippe, Jean-Paul Sartre, and Pierre Victor. *On a raison de se révolter*. Paris: Gallimard, 1974.

Gide, André. *Correspondance André Gide-Roger Martin du Gard*, Vol. i. Paris: Editions de la Pléiade, 1968.

————. *Littérature engagée*. Paris: Gallimard, 1950.

————. *Journal*. Paris: Bibliothèque de la Pléiade, 1951.

Ginsbourg, Ariel. *Nizan*. Paris: Editions Universitaires, 1966.

Goguel, François. *La Politique des partis sous la IIIe République*, 3rd ed. Paris: Editions du Seuil, n.d. (first published 1954).

Goldmann, Lucien. *Pour une Sociologie du roman*. Paris: Gallimard, 1964.

Grover, Frederic J. *Drieu la Rochelle and the Fiction of Testimony*. Berkeley: University of California Press, 1958.

Guissard, Lucien. *Emmanuel Mounier*. Paris: Editions Universitaires, 1962.

Gurvitch, Georges. *Les Tendances actuelles de la philosophie allemande*. Paris: J. Vrin, 1949.

Hamilton, Alastair. *The Appeal of Fascism*. New York: Avon, 1971.

Hughes, H. Stuart. *Consciousness and Society*. New York: Knopf, 1958.

————. *The Obstructed Path. French Social Thought in the Years of Desperation, 1930-1960*. New York: Harper and Row, 1968.

Isorni, Jacques. *Le Procès de Robert Brasillach*. 2nd ed. Paris: Flammarion, 1956.

Jaspers, Karl. *Psychopathologie générale*. Paris: Alcan, 1928 (translation revised by Paul Nizan and Jean-Paul Sartre).

Jeanson, Francis. *Sartre dans sa vie*. Paris: Editions du Seuil, 1974.

Johnston, William M. *The Austrian Mind*. Berkeley: University of California Press, 1972.

Kadushin, Charles. *The American Intellectual Elite*. Boston: Little, Brown, 1974.

Koestler, Arthur. *Darkness at Noon*. New York: Signet Books, 1960 (first published 1941).

Kohn-Etiemble, Jenine, ed. *226 Lettres inéditres de Jean Paulhan*. Paris: Klincksieck, 1975.

Lasch, Christopher. *The Agony of the American Left*. New York: Vintage Books, 1969.

————. *The New Radicalism in America, 1889-1963: The Intellectual as a Social Type*. New York: Knopf, 1965.

Leiner, Jacqueline. *Le Destin littéraire de Paul Nizan*. Paris: Klincksieck, 1970.

Lewis, David L. *Prisoners of Honor. The Dreyfus Affair*. New York: William Morrow, 1973.

Loubet del Bayle, Jean-Louis. *Les Non-Conformistes des années 30*. Paris: Editions du Seuil, 1969.

Macdonald, H. Malcolm, ed. *The Intellectual in Politics*. Austin: University of Texas Press, 1966.

Malraux, André. *Le Temps du mépris*. Paris: Gallimard, 1935.

Malraux, Clara. *Les Combats et les jeux (Le Bruit de nos pas, III)*. Paris: Grasset, 1969.

————. *Nos Vingt Ans (Le Bruit de nos pas, II)*. Paris: Grasset, 1966.

————. *Voici qui vient l'Eté (Le Bruit de nos pas, IV)*. Paris: Grasset, 1973.

Merleau-Ponty, Maurice. *Humanisme et terreur*. Paris: Gallimard, 1947.

Miquel, Pierre. *L'Affaire Dreyfus*. Paris: Presses Universitaires de France, 1968.

Moix, Candide. *La Pensée d'Emmanuel Mounier*. Paris: Editions du Seuil, 1960.

Mounier, Emmanuel. *Oeuvres*, Vol. IV, Paris: Editions du Seuil, 1963.

————. *Le Personnalisme*. Paris: Presses Universitaires de France, 1949.

Myrdal, Jan. *Confessions of a Disloyal European*. New York: Vintage Books, 1969.

Newfield, Jack. *A Prophetic Minority*. New York: Signet Books, 1966.

Niess, Robert J. *Julien Benda*. Ann Arbor: University of Michigan Press, 1956.

Nietzsche, Friedrich. *The Genealogy of Morals*. Francis Golffing, tr. New York: Doubleday Anchor Books, 1956.

Nizan, Paul. *Aden Arabie*. Paris: François Maspero, 1961 (first published 1931). This edition includes a long introduction by Jean-Paul Sartre.

———. *Antoine Bloyé*. Paris: Grasset, 1933.

———. *Le Cheval de Troie*. Paris: Gallimard, 1935.

———. *Les Chiens de garde*. Paris: Maspero, 1965 (first published 1932).

———. *La Conspiration*. Paris: Gallimard, 1968 (first published 1938).

———. *Les Matérialistes de l'Antiquité*. Paris: Maspero, 1968 (first published 1936).

———. *Paul Nizan, Intellectuel communiste*. J.-J. Brochier, ed. Paris: Maspero, 1967 (a valuable collection, with a biographical introduction). Second, enlarged, ed. in 2 vols. Paris: Maspero, 1970.

———. *Pour une Nouvelle Culture*. Susan Suleiman, ed. Paris: Grasset, 1971 (useful selection of articles and reviews published between 1930 and 1939).

Nolte, Ernst. *Three Faces of Fascism*. Leila Vennewitz, tr. New York: Holt, Rinehart, and Winston, 1966.

Novick, Peter. *The Resistance versus Vichy*. New York: Columbia University Press, 1968.

Orwell, George. *The Road to Wigan Pier*. London: Penguin Books, 1962 (first published 1937).

Parker, Emmett. *Albert Camus: The Artist in the Arena*. Madison: University of Wisconsin Press, 1965.

Plumyène, J., and R. Lasierra. *Les Fascismes français, 1923-1963*. Paris: Editions du Seuil, 1963.

Poster, Mark. *Existential Marxism in Postwar France: From*

Sartre to Althusser. Princeton: Princeton University Press, 1975.

Poulat, Emile. *Naissance des Prêtres-ouvriers*. Paris: Casterman, 1965.

Rabil, Albert, Jr. *Merleau-Ponty*. New York: Columbia University Press, 1967.

Redfern, W. D. *Paul Nizan. Committed Literature in a Conspiratorial World*. Princeton: Princeton University Press, 1972.

Rémond, René. *La Droite en France de 1815 à nos jours*. Paris: Aubier, 1954.

Rieff, Philip, ed. *On Intellectuals*. Garden City, New York: Doubleday, 1969 (important for the study of engagement; contains essays by Talcott Parsons, Edward Shils, J. P. Nettl, Stuart Samuels, and others).

Rogger, Hans, and Eugen Weber, eds. *The European Right: A Historical Profile*. Berkeley: University of California Press, 1965.

Rossi, A. (pseud. for A. Tasca). *Physiologie du Parti Communiste*. Paris: Self, 1948.

de Rougemont, Denis. *Politique de la personne. Problèmes, doctrines et tactique de la révolution personnaliste*. Paris: Editions "Je Sers," 1934.

Saint-Exupéry, Antoine de. *A Sense of Life*. Adrienne Foulke, tr. New York: Funk and Wagnalls Co., 1965.

Sartre, Jean-Paul. *Qu'est-ce que la littérature?* (*Situations* II). Paris: Gallimard, 1948.

Schalk, David L. *Roger Martin du Gard: The Novelist and History*. Ithaca: Cornell University Press, 1967.

Sérant, Paul. *Le Romantisme fasciste . . . ou l'oeuvre politique de quelques écrivains français*. Paris: Fasquelle, 1959.

Simon, Pierre-Henri. *L'Esprit et l'histoire*. Paris: Armand Colin, 1954.

Sorel, Georges. *Réflexions sur la violence*. Paris: Marcel Rivière, 1912.

Soucy, Robert. *Fascism in France. The Case of Maurice Barrès*. Berkeley: University of California Press, 1972.

Southworth, Herbert R. *Le Mythe de la croisade de Franco*. Paris: Ruedo iberico, 1964.

Spender, Stephen. *World Within World*. New York: Harcourt, Brace and Co., 1948.

Staude, John Raphael. *Max Scheler, 1874-1928*. New York: Free Press, 1967.

Steiner, George. *Language and Silence. Essays on Language, Literature and the Inhuman*. New York: Atheneum, 1967.

Stéphane, Roger. *Portrait de l'aventurier*. 2nd ed. Paris: Grasset, 1965.

Thiher, Allen. *Céline: The Novel as Delirium*. New Brunswick: Rutgers University Press, 1972.

Tucker, William R. *The Fascist Ego. A Political Biography of Robert Brasillach*. Berkeley: University of California Press, 1975.

Vailland, Roger. *Drôle de Jeu*. Paris: Bûchet-Chastel, 1945. English edition, *Playing for Keeps*, Gerard Hopkins, tr. Boston: Houghton Mifflin, 1948.

————. *Le Surréalisme contre la révolution*. Paris: Editions Sociales, 1948.

Vandromme, Pol. *Robert Brasillach. L'Homme et l'oeuvre*. Paris: Plon, 1956.

Wallraff, Charles F. *Karl Jaspers. An Introduction to His Philosophy*. Princeton: Princeton University Press, 1970.

Weber, Eugen. *Action Française*. Stanford: Stanford University Press, 1962.

Williams, Raymond. *Culture and Society, 1780-1950*. New York: Columbia University Press, 1958.

Winock, Michel. *Histoire politique de la revue "Esprit" 1930-1950*. Paris: Editions du Seuil, 1975.

Wood, Neal. *Communism and the British Intellectuals*. New York: Columbia University Press, 1959.

ARTICLES AND SHORTER PIECES

Acherson, Neal. "High on Guilt," *New York Review of Books* (August 1, 1968), p. 20.

Barillon, Raymond. "M. Jean-Paul Sartre et la Violence," *Le Monde hebdomadaire* (April 30–May 6, 1970), p. 6.

de Beauvoir, Simone. "Oeil pour oeil," *Les Temps modernes*, Vol. 1, No. 5 (February 1946), pp. 813–30.

Bédé, Jean-Albert. Review of *Paul Nizan*, by Ariel Ginsbourg, *Romanic Review*, Vol. LVIII, No. 4 (December 1967), pp. 310–13.

Benda, Julien. "Les Essais," review of *Socialisme fasciste*, by Drieu la Rochelle, *N.R.F.* (February 1935), pp. 295–96.

Blanzat, Jean. "Comptes Rendus," review of Drieu la Rochelle, *La Comédie de Charleroi, Europe*, No. 136 (April 15, 1934), pp. 595–96.

Brogan, Denis W. "Introduction," to *Encounters* (an anthology from the first ten years of *Encounter* magazine), Stephen Spender, Irving Kristol, Melvin J. Lasky, eds. London: Wiedenfeld and Nicolson, 1963, pp. xv–xxviii.

Brustein, Robert. "If an Artist Wants to be Serious and Respected *and* Rich, Famous and Popular, He is Suffering from Cultural Schizophrenia," *New York Times Magazine* (September 27, 1971), p. 89.

Cobb, Richard. "The Politics of Intransigence," *Times Literary Supplement* (January 23, 1976), p. 71.

Coser, Lewis. "Julien Benda—On 'Intellectual Treason,' " *Encounter* (April 1973), pp. 32–36.

Chomsky, Noam. "The Responsibility of Intellectuals," in *American Power and the New Mandarins*. New York: Vintage, 1969, pp. 323–66. Also in the *New York Review of Books* (February 23, 1967).

Curley, Arthur. Review of *Aden Arabie* by Paul Nizan, *Library Journal*, Vol. XCIII (May 15, 1968), p. 2000.

Davenport, Guy. Review of *Aden Arabie*, by Paul Nizan, *New York Times Book Review* (June 30, 1968), p. 10.

Desanti, Dominique. Review of *Les Ecrits de Sartre*, by Michel Contat and Michel Rybalka, *Le Monde hebdomadaire* (April 9–15, 1970), p. 13.

Domenach, Jean-Marie. "Le Malaise française," *Le Monde hebdomadaire* (November 13–19, 1969), p. 7.

Drieu la Rochelle, Pierre. "L'Homme mûr et le jeune homme," *N.R.F.* (February 1935), pp. 190-210.

———. "Le Monde pharisien," *N.R.F.* (August 1934), pp. 309-10.

———. "Unité Française et Unité Allemande," *Europe*, no. 133 (January 15, 1934), pp. 23-37.

Eliot, T. S. Review of *The Treason of the Intellectuals*, by Julien Benda, *New Republic* (December 12, 1928), pp. 105-7.

Eluard, Paul. Preface to *l'Honneur des poètes*, in *Oeuvres Complètes*, II. Paris: Gallimard, 1968.

"Un 'Engagement' gauchiste," *Le Monde hebdomadaire* (June 17-23, 1971), p. 8.

"L'Escalade de la haine," Editorial, *Le Monde hebdomadaire* (January 23-29, 1969), p. 1.

Esprit, Emmanuel Mounier, ed., No. 1 (October 1932), *et seq*.

Fernandez, Ramon. "Lettre ouverte à André Gide," *N.R.F.* (April 1934), pp. 703-8.

———. "Littérature et politique," *N.R.F.* (February 1935), pp. 285-91.

———. "Notes sur l'évolution d'André Gide," *N.R.F.* (July 1933), pp. 129-35.

Fisher, David James. "The Rolland-Barbusse Debate," *Survey*, No. 91/92 (Spring/Summer, 1974), pp. 121-59.

Gauss, Christian. "Introduction," to *The Prince*, by Machiavelli. New York: Mentor Classics, 1952, pp. 7-30.

Gide, André. "Feuillets," *N.R.F.* (May 1, 1933), pp. 720-27.

Girardet, Raoul. "Notes sur l'Esprit d'un fascisme français," *Revue Française de science politique*, Vol. 5, No. 3 (July-September, 1955), pp. 529-46.

Goldmann, Lucien. "Introduction aux premiers écrits de Georges Lukacs," *Les Temps modernes*, No. 195 (August 1962). Reprinted in Georges Lukacs, *La Théorie du roman* (Paris: Editions Gonthier, 1963), pp. 156-90.

Hellman, J. W. "Emmanuel Mounier: A Catholic Revolutionary at Vichy," *Journal of Contemporary History*, Vol. 8, No. 4 (October 1973), pp. 3-23.

Howe, Irving. "The New York Intellectuals," *Commentary*, Vol. 46, No. 4 (October 1968), pp. 29-51.

Jefferson, Carter. "Communism and the French Intellectuals, 1919-1923," *Comparative Studies in Society and History*, Vol. 11, No. 3 (June 1969), pp. 241-57.

Journal of Contemporary History, Vol. i, No. 2 (1966). Issue devoted to "Left-Wing Intellectuals Between the Wars."

Lalou, René. "Le Rôle social des écrivains," *Gavroche* (March 8, 1945), p. 1.

Landsberg, P.-L. "L'Acte philosophique de Max Scheler," *Recherches philosophiques*, Vol. vi (1936-1937), pp. 299-312.

———. "Réflexions sur l'engagement personnel," *Esprit*, No. 62 (November 1937), pp. 179-97.

Levey, Jules. "Georges Valois and the Faisceau: The Making and Breaking of a Fascist," *French Historical Studies*, Vol. viii, No. 2 (Fall 1973), pp. 279-304.

Loewenberg, Peter. "The Psychohistorical Origins of the Nazi Youth Cohort," *American Historical Review*, Vol. 76, No. 5 (December 1971), pp. 1457-1502.

———. "The Unsuccessful Adolescence of Heinrich Himmler," *American Historical Review*, Vol. 76, No. 3 (June 1971), pp. 612-41.

Lüthy, Herbert. "The French Intellectuals," in George B. de Huszar, ed., *The Intellectuals*. Glencoe: The Free Press, 1960.

Malraux, André. "Réponse à Trotsky," *N.R.F.* (April 1931), pp. 501-7.

———. "L'Art est une conquête," *Commune*, Nos. 13-14 (September-October 1934), pp. 68-71.

———. "L'Attitude de l'artiste," *Commune*, No. 15 (November 1934), pp. 166-74.

Maulnier, Thierry. "Reponse à Julien Benda," *La Nef*, No. 12 (November 1945), pp. 48-54.

Meriel, Denis. "Le Théatre," *N.R.F.* (December 1934), pp. 929-31.

Merleau-Ponty, M., and Jean-Paul Sartre. "Les jours de notre vie," *Les Temps modernes*, No. 51 (June 1950), pp. 1153-1168.

Miller, Karl. "Episodes in the Class War," *New York Review of Books* (November 15, 1973), pp. 25-28.

Le Monde (February 7, 1970). A special supplement dedicated to Robert Brasillach.

Mosse, George L. "Fascism and the Intellectuals," in S. J. Woolf, ed., *The Nature of Fascism*. New York: Random House, 1968, pp. 205-25.

Mount, Ferdinand. "A History of Grim Frivolities," *National Review* (April 13, 1973), pp. 425-26.

Nisbet, Robert A. "Subjective Si! Objective No!" *New York Times Book Review* (April 5, 1970), p. 36.

Nizan, Paul. "Les Conséquences du refus," *N.R.F.*, No. 231 (December 1932), pp. 806-11.

———. "Renaissance de la tragédie," *L'Humanité* (March 1, 1936), p. 6.

———. "Sindobad Tocikiston," *Europe*, No. 149 (May 15, 1935), pp. 73-99.

———. "Sur l'Humanisme," *Europe*, No. 151 (July 15, 1935), pp. 452-57.

O'Brien, Conor Cruise. "Journal de Combat," in C. C. O'Brien, *Writers and Politics*. London: Chatto and Windus, 1965, pp. 169-72.

Ory, Pascal. "Apologie pour un meurtre," *Le Monde* (February 6, 1975), p. 10.

Poirot-Delpech, Bertrand. Review of *Situations* x, by Jean-Paul Sartre, *Le Monde hebdomadaire* (January 22-28, 1976), p. 14.

Redfern, W. D. "A Vigorous Corpse: Paul Nizan and *La Conspiration*," *Romanic Review*, Vol. 59, No. 4 (December 1968), pp. 278-95.

Rolland, Romain. "Lénine: l'art et l'action," *Europe*, No. 133 (January 14, 1934), pp. 5-14.

————. Letters to Henri Barbusse, February and March 1922, in *Textes politiques, sociaux et philosophiques choisis*, Jean Albertini, ed. Paris: Editions Sociales, 1970, pp. 215, 232.

————. "Lettre ouverte à Gerhart Hauptmann," in R. Rolland, *Au-dessus de la Mêlée*. Paris: Ollendorff, 1915, pp. 6-8.

————. "Lettres à Staline," *L'Humanité* (July 22, 1935), p. 1.

————. "L'U.R.S.S. en a vu bien d'autres!," *L'Humanité* (January 18, 1937), p. 1.

Sartre, Jean-Paul. "Ce que je suis," *Le Nouvel Observateur* (June 23-July 27, 1975). An interview with Michel Contat, translated in an abridged version in the *New York Review of Books* (August 7, 1975), pp. 10-17.

————. "Jean-Paul Sartre Répond," *L'Arc*, No. 30 (1966), pp. 87-96. An interview with Bernard Pingaud.

————. Review of Paul Nizan, *La Conspiration*, in *Situations* i. Paris: Gallimard, 1947, pp. 26-30.

————. "Sartre Accuses the Intellectuals of Bad Faith," *New York Times Magazine* (October 17, 1971), pp. 38ff. An interview with John Gerassi.

————. "What's Jean-Paul Sartre Thinking Lately?," *Esquire* (December 1972), pp. 204ff. An interview with Pierre Bénichou.

Schalk, David L. "Birth of a Movement," *Journal of Social History*, Vol. 4, No. 1 (Fall 1970), pp. 88-94.

Schlumberger, Jean. "Note sur la politique," *N.R.F.* (December 1, 1934), pp. 866-71.

Solomon, Barbara Probst. Review of *Antoine Bloyé*, by Paul Nizan, *New York Times Book Review* (June 23, 1973), pp. 4-5.

Soucy, Robert. "Le Fascisme de Drieu la Rochelle," *Revue d'histoire de la Deuxième Guerre Mondiale*, No. 66 (April 1967), pp. 61-84.

————. "French Fascist Intellectuals in the 1930s: An Old New Left?," *French Historical Studies*, Vol. viii, No. 3 (Spring 1974), pp. 445-58.

Soucy, Robert. "The Nature of Fascism in France," in Nathanael Greene, ed. *Fascism. An Anthology*. New York: Crowell, 1968, pp. 275-300.

———. "Psycho-Sexual Aspects of the Fascism of Drieu la Rochelle," *The Journal of Psychohistory*, Vol. 4, No. 1 (Summer 1976), pp. 71-92.

———. "Romanticism and Realism in the Fascism of Drieu la Rochelle," *Journal of the History of Ideas*, Vol. 31, No. 1 (January-March 1970), pp. 69-90.

Steiner, George. "Georg Lukacs—A Preface," in Georg Lukacs, *Realism in our Time*, John and Necke Mander, trs. New York: Harper and Row, 1964, pp. 7-15.

———. "Preface," to J. S. McClelland, ed. *The French Right*. New York: Harper and Row, 1970, pp. 5-6.

Stone, Lawrence. "The Ninnyversity?," *New York Review of Books* (January 28, 1971), pp. 21-29.

Thibaudet, Albert. "Réflexions," *N.R.F.* (February 1931), pp. 247-54.

Tucker, William R. "Politics and Aesthetics: The Fascism of Robert Brasillach," *Western Political Quarterly*, Vol. xv, No. 4 (December 1962), pp. 605-17.

Unik, Pierre. "André Gide et la vérité révolutionnaire," *Commune*, Nos. 13-14 (September-October 1934), pp. 131-38.

Wesseling, H. L. "Engagement tegen wil en dank: Franse intellectuelen en de Dreyfus-affaire," *Tijdschrift voor Geschiedenis*, 87 (1974), pp. 410-24.

———. "Robert Brasillach en de verlokiing van het fascisme," *Tijdschrift voor Geschiedenis*, 88 (1975), pp. 1-4.

Wicker, Tom. "The Malaise Beyond Dissent," *New York Times* (March 12, 1967), p. E13.

Wolff, Kurt H. "For a Sociology of Evil," *Journal of Social Issues*, Vol. 25, No. 1 (1969), pp. 111-25.

———. "The Intellectual: Between Culture and Politics," *International Journal of Contemporary Sociology*, Vol. 8, No. 1 (January 1971), pp. 13-34.

UNPUBLISHED MATERIALS

Chambat, Pierre. *Julien Benda, 1867-1956*. Thesis for the *Doctorat d'Etat ès Sciences Politiques*, Paris, 1976, 4 volumes.

Hellering, Andrea. *The Dump Johnson Movement, 1967-1968*. Senior Thesis, Vassar College, Poughkeepsie, New York, 1976.

Hoberman, John M. *The Psychology of the Collaborator in the Norwegian Novel*, Ph.D. Dissertation, Department of Scandinavian Languages and Literatures, University of California, Berkeley, 1975.

————. "Sympathy for the Devil: Ideological Conflict Among Literary Intellectuals in Liberated France," paper presented at the Third Annual Conference on Twentieth-Century Literature, University of Louisville, Kentucky, February 28, 1975.

Wasserman, Manuèle. *Artists in Politics in Nineteenth-Century France*, Ph.D. Dissertation, Department of History, Columbia University, New York, 1977.

Index

◊◊◊◊◊◊◊◊◊

Library of Congress Cataloging in Publication Data

Schalk, David L.
  The spectrum of political engagement

  Bibliography: p.
  Includes index.
  1. French prose literature—20th century—History
and criticism.   2. Authors, French—20th century—
Political activity.   3. Philosophy, French—20th century.   4. France—Politics and government—20th century.   5. France—Intellectual life.   I. Title.
PQ629.S3   843′.9′120931   78-70318
ISBN 0-691-05275-1